BRITH EMETH

IN MEMORY OF

[illegible]

PRESENTED BY

BRITH EMETH P & T A

SO STRANGE MY PATH

SO STRANGE MY PATH

A Spiritual Pilgrimage

by

ABRAHAM CARMEL

BLOCH PUBLISHING COMPANY
New York

Library of Congress Card Number: 64:17487

PRINTED IN THE UNITED STATES OF AMERICA

Dedicated to All Those
who helped me
along my Path

"... We therefore hope in Thee, O Lord our God, that we may speedily behold the glory of Thy might, when Thou wilt remove the abominations from the earth, and the idols will be utterly cut off, when the world will be perfected under the kingdom of the Almighty, and all the children of flesh will call upon Thy name, . . . and know that unto Thee every knee must bow, every . . . let them all accept the yoke of Thy kingdom and do Thou reign over them speedily, and for ever and ever. For the kingdom is Thine, and to all eternity Thou wilt reign in glory; as it is written in Thy Law: The Lord shall reign for ever and ever. And it is said, And the Lord shall be king over all the earth. In that day shall the Lord be One, and his name One."

From the daily recited closing prayer
"Aleinu". (1) *

* For reference to indices, please turn to page 236.

Contents

1

Childhood Influences

"Just as the twig is bent the tree's inclined."

POPE

"And God said to Avrom, go forth from your land, from your birthplace and from your father's house, to the land I will show thee."

GENESIS, 12, 1. (2)

Preface

to the Second Edition

Since the first edition of *So Strange My Path* was published in 1960, we have witnessed many changes in the religious world.

A new tolerance, born of understanding, is evident in the attitude of men of different faiths, in their relationships with one another.

Much of the credit for this, is due to the late Pope John XXIII who, by his universal outlook, did so much to discredit bigotry, and foster brotherhood. He was a genuine friend of the Jewish people, and we pray that his sweet memory may be cherished by future generations of Jews and Gentiles alike.

The recent visit to Israel by his illustrious successor, Pope Paul VI augurs well for a continued improvement in the hitherto unhappy relationship between the Church and the Synagogue. The fruits of the Ecumenical Council have yet to be seen, but a clear repudiation of anti-Semitism, and the theological teachings which so tragically helped to breed it, would have a significant impact upon the Christian World.

Meanwhile, the Jewish community has its domestic problems. Our immediate danger stems less from anti-Semitism, than from the arch-enemy, assimilation!

At least one third of our brethren in America are in danger of being lost to their people, and heritage. Among our Jewish students, the peril is particularly grave. Most teenagers leave high school for the campus, with barely more than a Bar Mitzvah knowledge of Judaism.

Very many of their parents belong to the "lost generation."

In the Author's respectful submission, there is only one solution to this critical problem, viz.: Jewish Education.

We must spend less on luxurious synagogues, and considerably more on Jewish schools. Otherwise, the former will be empty tombs, by 1984!

Our responsibilities were seldom so overwhelming, but our opportunities were never as great.

With faith and courage, let us build a new future for our children. May they find a true pride in their heritage, and a purposeful life of service in the interests of humanity.

Finally, the Author, who worked for two years in Israel, expresses the hope that all those who can, will journey to the land of their fathers, and receive the inspiration that it alone can give.

"If I forget thee, O Jerusalem, let my tongue cleave to the roof of my mouth; if I remember not thee, O Zion, let my right hand forget her cunning."

New York, 1964
5724

ABRAHAM CARMEL

FOR a Christian to become a Jew is not unheard of, though fairly rare, and in most cases is brought about through mixed marriages. But for a priest of the Roman Catholic Church to embrace Judaism—and purely for Judaism's own sake—that, surely, must be an occurrence almost, if not wholly, unique. This, then, is the strange story of one who, by ancestry a Scot and an Anglican, forsook the Established Church for Rome, served as a Catholic Priest, and at last found his spiritual home within the Jewish fold.

Inevitably, so spectacular a transition has occasioned considerable comment, sometimes incredulous, sometimes mildly ribald. To take just one example, even my friend Hubert S. Banner, who has been of much assistance to me in the preparation of this book, once informed me, with a twinkle in his eye, that there had been a popular song at the time of the First World War entitled "The only Yiddische Scotchman in the Irish Fusiliers"!

As far as possible, I shall reduce to a minimum the mass of tedious irrelevant details of childhood and youth which so many autobiographers thrust upon their long-suffering readers. Yet there were personalities, incipient traits of character, early trends, and little episodes which undoubtedly had their significance in the light of what followed, and some of those I certainly must notice if my later history is to be understood.

I was born Kenneth Charles Cox in 1911 at Greenwich, London. My parents, members of industrialist and property-owning families, died when I was quite young, leaving me to be brought up by elderly guardians. Mr. and Mrs. Jackman, whom I could not have loved more had I been their own son. I remember how, when I was about eleven years old, Mrs. Jackman fell very seriously ill. Had she died, I should have been in sore straits indeed. I prayed over her with all the fervour of what I undoubtedly was—a precociously religious-minded child. The next day my guardian rose from her bed, restored to health, and I need scarcely add that this prompt answer to my prayer went far to confirm me in my devotional bent. Clearly, Heaven had its eye upon me!

I described myself just now as "precociously religious-minded". At the age of eight I loved to dress up on Sunday afternoons in multi-coloured oddments of clothing, commandeer an arm-chair to serve as pulpit, and gather my doting elders together to hear me hold forth on some Bible story or supposed moral issue. I knew literally dozens of the Psalms by heart and could reel off whole chapters of the Prophets or New Testament at the drop of a hat. Study was an obsession with me. From the age of ten until I left school I collected every English and Scripture prize available.

Nevertheless, I enjoyed games like any other healthy boy; I sang in the church choir, but I also put in four years in the Boy Scouts and got nothing but pleasure out of them. And although peaceably inclined, I did on one occasion fight a full-scale battle which astonished my schoolfellows. When they saw the school bully slink off with a discoloured eye they could hardly believe it was the swotting, scripture-reciting boy who had administered the much-needed chastisement. My stock fairly sky-rocketed from that hour.

If I had to produce a comparative evaluation of the people who most influenced me in those early years I'm sure the list would be headed by that sprightly, morale-boosting octogenarian my grandfather, who, with a view to easing the somewhat tight financial situation, came to live with us while I was still at school. I shall never forget my first meeting with Grandpa. I had been told that he was eighty, but here was a ramrod-straight, immaculate figure, beaming like one of Dickens' Cheerible brothers and looking, with his bright cord waistcoat and gleaming watch-chain, like a living symbol of better days. I would not have thought that he was a day over sixty.

But it was at sixty that he had retired after being estate manager to various titled families. On his dressing-table was a case of magnificent gold tiepins presented to him by members of the various families he had served.

Among his most cherished memories was that of holding Princess (later Queen) Alexandra in his arms after she had suffered a fall in the hunting field. His knowledge of the private lives of certain noble, and even royal, personages would have provided material for an interesting book.

Retiring, as I have said, at sixty, Grandpa had gone North to help one of my uncles found a motor works. All his life he had lived with horses around him, till it was said he could almost converse with them. But horses were on their way out and cars on their way in, so he adapted himself accordingly and invested his considerable savings in my uncle's newly established business.

Grandpa was generous. Whenever he lost his temper, which was fairly often, he invariably made amends with a pound note, worth more than five dollars at the time. "Go and enjoy yourself, boy!" he would say. And I am sure he meant it, though unfortunately I never seemed to have either the nerve or the imagination to put his injunction satisfactorily into effect. He himself had lived an exemplary life, but appeared to think—and perhaps he was right—that a wild fling would do me more good than harm.

Each summer, up to the age of eighty-six, the grand old man would set out, alone and robustly independent, on a holiday jaunt covering never less than five hundred miles. He was loved and respected by all who knew him. And when at last he died, in his ninety-third year, a large and distinguished concourse assembled for the funeral in his beloved Norfolk. He had asked that his favourite hymn should be sung—it was my grandmother's favourite also—and I saw to it that his wishes were carried out.

He was deeply religious, and it may have been partly because of my own religious trend that from the very outset he took a special interest in me. Moreover, he apparently formed a high opinion of my scholastic possibilities and was keenly anxious to see me given good opportunities to progress. The greater part of his money being invested in my uncle's firm, he begged the family to co-operate, but all to no purpose. So it was clear that for any further advancement I had to rely upon my own scholarship-earning capacity, and happily this did come to the rescue. In all the ways that lay within his power, however, Grandpa was a constant inspiration and stimulus to me, and after his death, following twelve years of happy association, his influence was never entirely to forsake me.

Another outstanding factor in my early life was the friendship of the Church of England rector of our parish, the Reverend F. W. Head. This former Fellow and Tutor of Emmanuel College, Cambridge, and chaplain to King George V, was a tower of spiritual strength. As padre to one of the Guards regiments, he had been awarded the Military Cross for rescuing men under fire in World War I. Physically frail, he was yet a moral and spiritual giant. On leaving the Army, he had gone to a parish of nearly 30,000 souls, and within two years he had filled to overflowing a previously half-empty church. Although required several times a year to preach before the Royal Family at Sandringham or Windsor, his greatest delight was to lecture or preach to working-class congregations. His prestige was tremendous, but he remained simple and free from ambition. A great scholar, he wore his learning modestly. History was his special subject, and he was the author of a noted work *The Fall of the Stuarts*. Eventually he went to Melbourne, Australia, as

Archbishop, and there, alas, he was killed in a motor accident.

I can still see Mr. Head as he stood on a table outside his church, answering question after question on religious or moral problems put to him by non-churchgoers. It would have required a strong missionary spirit in any Church of England clergyman to have done as much, but in a University-conditioned clergyman who regularly preached before the Royal Family, it was indeed a phenomenon. Small wonder that he was deeply revered by one and all, irrespective of class or creed. One thing he frequently denounced was the habit of the newly rich of flaunting their wealth before the eyes of the poor. For although he came of a very distinguished family and had married a daughter of a millionaire family, he remained truly humble and detested any form of ostentation, himself neither owning a car nor maintaining more than the minimum of servants at the rectory. It is good for a boy to have a guide to whom he can look with genuine faith and admiration, and this down-to-earth parson I venerated with all my heart.

Looking back, it seems to me that it was when I sang in the parish choir, carried away by the beauty and dignity of the services, that I began to feel an ever-increasing desire to make the ministry my life's work. Perhaps the seed of that yearning had been dormant within me since very early days, as witness my make-believe sermons to the household as a child. But of this I am sure: my leaning towards Holy Orders was powerfully moulded and given direction by the influence and example of those two men of whom I have just written—my grandfather and Mr. Head. And it may well have been reinforced by a saying of my schoolmaster when I was quite a small boy; an utterance I never forgot. "Aim at the stars," he said, "and nothing lower."

Whatever the origins of that leaning, it became a positive fixation. At school one day our English master asked us all in turn what we wanted to be when we grew up. The hasty answers he received covered the usual small-boy choice—"engine-driver", "policeman", "sailor", and all the rest. When it came to my turn, however, I simply blurted out, "I should like to be a clergyman." The entire class rocked with laughter and the master joined in. When at last the effect of my bombshell had subsided the master, possibly a little ashamed of his participation in the derision, congratulated me on my courage, though he added a warning that the clergy, despite their long, arduous years of study and training, were paid less generously than a postman.

It took me a couple of years to live down that rash avowal of my ambition. Whenever I committed some misdemeanour, however trivial, my sacerdotal aspirations would be cast in my teeth. "Parson" became my nickname, and it was a term of opprobrium. It soon came to be a recognized game in the playground to push me into one of the privies and force me to perform some disgustingly dirty action. Well knowing how I hated such filth, my schoolfellows took an unholy delight in my embarrassment, and the more I protested, the more they goaded me. In short, my life was made a veritable hell for me until at last the other boys came to realize that my determination was not to be broken. Furthermore, the headmaster had apparently been taking quiet note of these goings-on, for when it came to writing my testimonial he expressed gratification at what he termed my moral strength.

I was fourteen years old, I remember, when my potential aptitude for a clerical career was put to a practical test. A boy of my acquaintance was going around denying the existence of God to any who would give an ear to his adolescent vapourings. I felt impelled to answer him and, without the slightest previous preparation, I found myself giving this boy in a simple form the very arguments which philosophers have been wont to propound in far more elaborate style.

The liner *Queen Mary* had then recently been built on the Clyde, and I asked my friend to think of that gigantic ocean greyhound. I pointed out to him that in the first place designers were needed to conceive even the very notion of such a vessel. Next, draftsmen had to plan in minute detail every part of her. Materials had to be brought together, skilfully fashioned into perfect shape, and finally fitted. That was by no means all, however, I went on. Thousands of people were required to man the ship and, above all, the guiding hand of the captain was essential on the bridge. I asked the boy to imagine a situation in which, while in mid-ocean, all the crew were removed from the liner. How far, I asked, would she travel in safety? The chances of her floating on her own into New York harbour were one in countless millions. But the *Queen Mary*, I pointed out, huge though she was, was no more than a speck of dust in comparison with the extent of the universe. It was contrary to all reason to imagine that this vast machine, moving with incredible regularity and precision, could either come into existence or continue in motion without a mind to design it, a power to create it, and a perpetual influence to keep it in being.

I am glad to say that these homely arguments left my friend convinced. If I have related this incident at some length, it is because I feel it may perhaps help to explain how it came about that only two years later I found myself addressing a congregation of more than three hundred adults on the Ten Commandments and was honoured with a warm invitation to pay a return visit. And a year after that, like so many other young zealots, I held forth in Hyde Park, London, taking as my subject "Return to God". I thoroughly enjoyed this experience, especially the heckling, giving me, as it did, a good opportunity for telling retorts.

Although I had won a good scholarship, it was decided that it would be better for me to postpone further study for a couple of years and in the meantime to go into commercial life and gain a little experience of the practical world. So I obtained employment in a large tobacco firm and was placed in the sales department.

Before I go on to touch upon my life in this new environment, however, I would like to mention one very remarkable circumstance of my childhood—remarkable because I have never yet been able to account for it satisfactorily, and have been driven to wonder whether it could conceivably have been the germ of that powerful spiritual urge which, many years later, was to reshape the entire course of my life. The circumstances in question were simply this: from almost as far back as I can remember, whenever I saw a Jew I felt an affinity with him and a strong desire to become acquainted with him. Not that I came under Jewish influence of any sort or description; indeed, I cannot recall any Jewish person or institution with which I had any kind of connection during the first thirteen years of my life. Yet there the feeling was, inexplicable on any rational basis. I have sometimes thought it might perhaps be partially traced to my realization, beneath the surface of my boyish Christian fervour, that Jesus had been a Jew and practised the Jewish religion, particularly when taken in conjunction with a frequent saying of one valued family friend: "I wonder why we don't go to Synagogue as Jesus did?"

I enjoyed my spell of work in the tobacco firm. The Managing Director, though a somewhat terrifying character, was a model of impartial justice in any dispute which arose. As for the other directors, they appeared to recognize in me a young man of a stamp somewhat different from the majority of their subordinates, and they grew into the habit of entrusting me with a variety of special jobs. It was in connection with one of these commissions that I made an unfortunate blunder and, at the same time, had my eyes opened to certain matters hitherto undreamed of in an unsophisticated youth's philosophy. One day one of the younger directors, happening to pass me in the hall, hurriedly asked me to get him a shade. Presuming for no adequate reason that it was a perambulator shade he wanted, I ordered one accordingly, only to discover when the thing arrived that what he really required was a lampshade. Naturally I was very annoyed at my own stupidity, but my fellow workers evidently thought the incident excruciatingly funny, and I could not imagine why until it was explained to me that the director in question was a well-known employer of birth-control techniques.

The firm had a concert party, which used to go to various places at week-ends, giving concerts in aid of charity. Singing had always been, and still is, my favourite hobby; even today I spend my free day taking lessons from a professor of singing. Naturally enough I joined the concert party, and here again I was to learn some of the more startling facts of life. On one occasion we visited a village in Surrey to help some charitable function. The feelings of the "unsophisticated youth" can be better imagined than described when he discovered that several members of the party remained behind to spend the night with someone else's wife or husband as the case might be. . . .

During this commercial interlude, matters in the home parish had undergone a drastic change. My friend and mentor Mr. Head had left to take up the Melbourne Archbishopric, and in consequence I could no longer avail myself of his invaluable guidance. His successor, although a man of fine character and the best intentions, was not blessed with the former rector's dynamic personality and relentless drive. Within six months the congregation fell off by 50 per cent and after a year the parish was no better than mediocre.

It was at precisely this point, when spiritual aid and sage counsel were so conspicuously lacking, that I came most to need them. I was now nearing eighteen and superintendent of the parish Sunday School, but I was plunging more and more deeply into one of those religious crises so common in the lives of adolescents—a malady one might also describe as a spiritual chicken-pox.

To be specific, I had become painfully aware that all was not well in the Protestant camp. Authorities were contradicting one another and there was much heresy in high places. It was estimated that there were in active existence—and competition—no less than two hundred and fifty forms of Christian faith, and one heard it jokingly said that America had a religion for each citizen! No wonder, one felt, if in the mission field the poor native was sorely perplexed, told by each of a baker's dozen of different missionaries that his own particular brand of Christianity was the one and only authentic one and that others were accordingly false: what was one to believe?

Even the Anglican bishops were divided among themselves. There was, for example, the abortive attempt on the part of the Venerable Archbishop Davidson to pilot the New Prayer Book through the Houses of Parliament. After spending long and laborious years on its preparation, he was defeated—mainly through the efforts of Sir Joynson Hicks, protagonist of the Low Church party. It was a cruel blow to the old warrior of Lambeth, and even now it seems quite absurd to me that the voting on a New Prayer Book should have been at the tender mercies of Members of Parliament who might have been Nonconformists, Roman Catholics, Jews, Agnostics, or, for that matter, out-and-out Atheists.

There were, no doubt, many Anglican worshippers who could attend a church service, gain a measure of inspiration and contentment from its mere solemnity and beauty, and depart in peace, oblivious to the theological implications involved. For my part, however, I wanted an *authority*—an authority which could and would tell me clearly what to believe. The various sections of the Established Church taught conflicting doctrines about one and the same person—Jesus. Who was right and who was wrong?

Since the days of the Reformation the English Church had been founded on compromise, and perhaps this was a natural enough development in view of the fact that compromise is a quality inherent in the British people. Henry VIII had not intended changing the doctrines of the Church.

He had been content with casting off the yoke of eternal authority as formerly exercised over the country by Rome.

Under Edward VI, and later under Elizabeth I, various doctrinal changes had, it was true, come into being. The Mass, for example, had become an "abomination", and certain other sacraments had been abandoned. The more severe and radical religious reforms, however, had come only gradually until at last, under Oliver Cromwell, but little of the old faith was left. The stress now lay more upon the Bible and less upon the Catholic sacramental system and dogma.

For several centuries thereafter the English Church had been what might be termed Low Church or Evangelical. The externals of worship had been but few and of the simplest. But in the nineteenth century much of the old Catholic faith had been revived by the Oxford Movement, and the High Churchmen, or Ritualists, as they sometimes were harshly called, had persevered in their efforts despite all legal opposition. Great names such as Newman, Pusey, and Faber had signalized the revival in English Catholicism or, to give it its later title, Anglo-Catholicism. The Anglo-Catholic party in the Church of England had gone forward steadily from then on, gaining strength with every decade, until it had become what it is today, probably the most powerful influence in the Established Church, counting many bishops in its ranks.

To return, however, to my own spiritual difficulties. I truly loved the Anglican Church, with its admirable body of clergy, who were, for the most part, gentlemen, scholars, and faithful shepherds. The profound impress laid upon my early years under the rector I had so greatly revered could not easily be destroyed. But however much the Church had meant to me, and still did, the confusion of voices in what had, alas, become a religious Babel, distressed me beyond measure. For I had, after all, become a religious *thinker*, and it mattered very much to me whether a thing was right or wrong, not only in matters of conduct, but also in matters of belief. We live by what we believe, and I could not but feel strongly that right or true belief was absolutely essential to a true life. In the spiritual crisis in which I now found myself a church, the doctrines of which were based on compromise, could no longer satisfy me. I wanted Truth, unvarnished, authoritative, and clearly defined beyond possibility of error.

Was Protestantism, I asked myself, just a phase in history —intended, perhaps, to purify Christianity—or was it simply passing through a bad stage and might later emerge revitalized? The trouble was, I could not afford to wait and see. My overmastering dissatisfaction and frustration insisted upon two qualities which the Established Church so conspicuously lacked—authority and vitality.

No, there was no longer any escaping the staggering fact that slowly but very surely I was moving away from Protestant Christianity. . . .

2

Search for a Faith

"Myself when young did eagerly frequent
Doctor and Saint, and heard great argument
About it and about: but evermore
Came out by the same door where in I went."
Rubáiyát of Omar Khayyám, EDWARD FITZGERALD

"A man cuts down a cedar . . . He takes part of it and warms himself, he kindles a fire and bakes bread, then he makes a god, worships it, he moulds an image, and prostrates himself before it."

ISAIAH, 44, 13–19. (3)

DRIVEN by my desperate urge to find an anchor of faith, I began to travel all over London, listening to the famous preachers of the day. Nowadays when, oratorically speaking, there is so sore a famine in the land, it is difficult to realize that in the thirties great preachers were in abundance. These things seem to go in cycles. Today there is scarcely a great orator among all the denominations; and what is worse, there are no great leaders either. "The hungry sheep look up and are not fed." In those days, on the contrary, I could have the choice of a dozen really outstanding spiritual giants.

The late Dr. Ernest Barnes, the Bishop of Birmingham, for example, was drawing vast congregations whenever he preached in London. It so happened that I was in St. Paul's Cathedral on that famous, or notorious, Sunday morning when the noted physicist and—in Anglo-Catholic eyes—sceptic and heretic, was publicly denounced by a body of that party led by a City of London canon. Arriving at the foot of the pulpit, and making the sign of the Cross in what seemed to me a very aggressive manner for representatives of a Protestant Church, the delegation of wrath read out their denunciation, about turned, and stalked out. Moreover, in an evident desire to be posthumously revenged upon Luther they even pinned a statement of their indignation on the cathedral door.

Their seats were quickly filled by worshippers standing in the aisles, and the learned scientist from the Midlands proceeded with his sermon. Contrary to his usual line of discourse, it contained no refutation of Christian doctrine. The

Trinity, the Virgin Birth, and the Resurrection were left in peace for once, and instead he treated us to a talk about the planets which would have done credit to the lecture room of a physics faculty. He ended by consoling us with the profound observation that the all-wise Creator would not suffer to perish that which was worth preserving. Why any man should have to wear mitre and gaiters to arrive at such a penetrating conclusion has always puzzled me.

It must, of course, be borne in mind, however, that Ramsay MacDonald was Prime Minister when his Lordship was elected; and as he was a particularly non-conforming Nonconformist, I suspect he wanted to give Canterbury a run for its money. This he surely succeeded in doing. Bishop Barnes proved more than a headache; he was a positive nightmare to a whole succession of Primates. And in the Church of England it requires almost an Act of God to remove a bishop, or even a dean, from his throne or stall. So long as he lives a respectable life, he is free to preach heresy until the cows come home. Needless to add that were he a Roman prelate or lesser light, far from awaiting the return of the cows, a papal bull would in double quick time chase him into the wilderness, if not right into the pit of unquenchable flames.

It may have been that Dr. Barnes and his friends of the Modern Churchmen's Union caused the sceptics of the day to vouchsafe a limited approval to the Church. But they disturbed thousands in their belief, and I was one of those disturbed. At that time a fierce struggle was in progress between religion and science. Today we hear less of that struggle for the simple reason that fundamental religion has more than held its own in the conflict.

A series of highly significant discoveries by such learned men as Sir Richard Kenyon have gone far to restore public confidence in the Bible. Scientists are no longer so strongly inclined as was the case half a century ago, or even less, to clothe themselves with infallibility. They realize now that there are many crucial problems upon which they can throw little or no light. True, they can observe phenomena, but they are not always able to account for it. The mystery of life is still a major mystery. We can observe growth and experience its effects, but what precisely is life? Already many previously unchallenged theories of science have been seriously modified, while some have been abandoned altogether. Greatly as one has to admire the achievements of science, it must be recognized that its limitations are very real. And speaking personally, there have been certain findings of the scientists which I cannot help hoping may yet be disproved. It was good news to me, for example, when I learned that science was becoming a little more conservative in its attitude towards the Darwinian theory of the evolution of man. After all, we already have so much to humiliate us that it seems a great pity to grasp at unnecessary insults, such as the thesis that we and the apes have descended from a common ancestry.

Most modern scientists recognize clear indications of intelligence in the workings of the universe, and philosophers are agreed that intelligence can proceed only from an intelligent source. In Nature, moreover, the scientists are able to observe millions of inimitable laws which give order in an incomparable way to the human beings, beasts, birds, and plants that inhabit the earth. The laws are also easily discernible in the universe at large, but again philosophy tells us that there can be no laws without a law-giver. Everything we see around us is caused by something or somebody, and in the final issue we have to trace it back to an "uncaused cause", called by some scientists the First Cause. The author, together with all religious-minded, calls it God.

Furthermore, the archaeologists have recently performed yeomen service in the cause of religious belief. To take but one example, our grandparents were taught to scoff at the biblical account of the destruction of Jericho. A few years ago, however, when the remains of Jericho were discovered, it was found that the walls had indeed been thrown down flat, and all within them was seen to be in a charred condition, thus completely vindicating the scriptural story.

Man, when faced with the most serious crises of life, finds science small comfort; it is then that he realizes the need of that consolation which religion, queen of the sciences, alone can give. The discovery by science of atomic energy, for instance, is in itself neither good nor bad. Like most inanimate things, it is neutral. It is the use to which men put their intelligence, the objectives in pursuit of which they exercise their will, that render them good or bad. Atomic power can either give light and heat or it can extinguish an entire population. The good or ill resides, not in the atom, but in the mind and will of man. If religion and science will only walk hand in hand, their partnership can save civilization. Otherwise—and this is a sober truth—we shall be utterly destroyed before the twenty-first century shall have dawned. . . .

At the time of which I am writing, much controversy centred around apparent discrepancies between the time-span covered by the process of Creation, as given in the Scriptures and the conclusions of geologists regarding the age of our planet. Today, of course, those differences no longer worry us. It has come to be clearly realized by scientist and biblical scholar alike that the Bible is not, and never was intended to be, a text-book of science. It is a message from the Creator to His creatures. The major and essential truths of Holy Writ, and particularly of the Book of Genesis, are that the universe was brought into being out of nothing by a Supreme Being who Himself had no beginning, but had always existed of Himself; that man was formed by God, and that at some particular point of time God infused into man's body a soul which is immortal; and that the human race has a common ancestry and a purpose decreed by God.

Provided those essential truths are respected, it surely can be of little consequence how the various processes developed or what duration of time may have been involved in their development. Science can but observe and record certain phenomena; it cannot provide the reason underlying them. That is the function of Divine Revelation, and without that Divine Revelation religion is meaningless.

And the arguments which apply to science apply also to philosophy. The philosophers of Ancient Greece travelled a long distance in the direction of truth, but they stopped short at the essential point where man needed clear guidance. Aristotle and Plato undoubtedly prepared the path for true and complete philosophy, but that was all. Philosophy can supply certain material answers to difficult problems, but religion must complete the work of philosophy even as it completes that of science.

These thoughts pursued one another round and round in my mind without end as, following my visit to St. Paul's, I reflected upon the interruption of Dr. Barnes' sermon by the Anglo-Catholic delegation and the modifying effect which, presumably, it had produced upon his "heretical" utterances. My overwhelming feeling was that not here, at all events, was to be found the clear, authoritative, vital Truth I so earnestly sought. . . .

Another of the famous contemporary preachers whom I went to hear at St. Paul's was Dean Inge. Like his friend, George Bernard Shaw, he lived to the ripe age of ninety. Nor could his longevity by any means be attributed to an optimistic temperament, for it was not for nothing that Ralph Inge had earned the sobriquet of "The Gloomy Dean". He never tired of predicting failure and disaster for civilization. He became the veritable British Jeremiah; and although no orator in the commonly accepted use of the word, he could always be sure of a large congregation, attracted by his biting satire and cryptic comments on the signs of the times. He wrote volumes on Plato and other philosophers, but whether he contributed anything new to philosophical thought is fiercely disputed. I can only record, for what it may be worth, that his jeremiads contributed nothing whatsoever towards the solution of those problems by which I was beset.

Then there was the Bishop of London, Dr. Winnington Ingram, whose ever-smiling countenance and somewhat impish manner presented a fundamental contrast with the disposition of his dyspeptic aide, the "gloomy dean". Dr. Ingram had previously been Bishop of Stepney, where he had greatly endeared himself to the working population of East London. Whenever he was to preach either at St. Paul's or at Westminster Abbey, a queue extending the whole way round the circumference of the building was to be seen long before the hour of the service. But here also I found only disappointment.

I next joined the throng to hear Dr. Dinsdale Young at the Westminster Central Hall, and he might easily have been Wesley reincarnated as he preached to a congregation of three thousand each Sunday evening. His manner was dynamic, and with his long, snow-white hair he cast a spell over the vast gathering. He resembled one of the Old Testament prophets, who, exhorting men to return to God, thundered dire warnings of impending doom. But despite the profundity of Dr. Young's sermons and their richness, both in language and in content, warnings of impending doom were not that which I so sorely needed. I continued my search.

My search took me to sit beneath the pulpits of such men as the great Temple, Archbishop of Canterbury; Downey, the Ciceronian Bishop of Liverpool; the unusually ascetic Cardinal Bourne at Westminster Cathedral; and a variety of other priests, less ascetic perhaps, but very convincing, though apart from these I left the idea of investigating Roman Catholicism for the time being in abeyance.

I went also to hear the Reverend Dick Sheppard, who was packing out St. Martin-in-the-Fields with his heartrending appeals for love and peace. A terrible sufferer from asthma, which shook his health to pieces, he carried on until completely overcome by exhaustion. His religious broadcasts were listened to by millions of non-churchgoers. He made no profession of being a learned theologian and he had no oratorical tricks up his sleeve. He simply preached himself over the ledge of his pulpit and into the hearts of his great congregations. His words could have penetrated marble, and even the most irreligious would go to hear him and come away softened in heart. If he had any secret at all, it was the simple secret of sincerity, springing from a love of humanity that had no limits. And still I wanted more even than that. . . .

It is not to be thought, by the way, that I restricted my research to the Christian groups. As some people find their outlet for a studious bent in science, music, art or some other channel, so I, from my earliest days, had sought to achieve a grasp of religious thought and spiritual values. In fact, comparative religion had always been my very special hobby, and as the years went by I had been gradually accumulating a knowledge and experience of the subject which must have been exceptional at my age. Now, in my sincere desire to arrive at Absolute Truth, I intensified my research into the territory of every faith which could lay claim to any degree of authority or influence, and the farther I progressed in my investigation, the more I was struck by the fact of how few Christians realize that there are many great and worthy religions in the world beside their own.

There was, for instance, Judaism. I had read in the newspapers that Rabbi Dr. Mattuck, of the Liberal Jewish Synagogue, preaching in North-West London, was attracting large gatherings to hear his eloquent appeals on behalf of his persecuted co-religionists in Nazi Germany and his warnings of the Nazi menace, which so few people in England had fully grasped at that time. I went to hear him, and for six months thereafter, at considerable inconvenience, I continued my attendance. This, had I but known it, was actually a false step in my search, and much was to happen before I was able to rectify it. The services seemed to me to be very similar to those in a Protestant church, the surroundings were, even to my untutored eye, very un-Jewish, and I felt that even the preacher had nothing to offer—not even Judaism! The trouble with me, though I had no means of knowing it at the time, was my ignorance of the fact that there exists a great gulf between Liberal or Reform Judaism and Orthodox Judaism, a difference that can hardly be appreciated by anybody who has not experienced the Orthodox way of life, which was not to be my portion for several years to come.

The two ways of life, that of the Liberal Jew and that of the Orthodox, are poles apart, and I feel bound to say that the Liberals have nothing whatever to offer that cannot be found in certain forms of Christianity, such as, for example, Unitarianism. They, as well as the Reform Jews, had rejected much of the tradition of Judaism as derived from the Bible. They took the attitude that modern conditions rendered the observance of many of the laws impracticable. Among other fundamental and radical changes, they rejected the dietary laws and most of the laws regarding observance of Sabbath; their Judaism was, in fact, very anaemic.

These matters, however, were at that time, as I have said, beyond my ken, and there were factors also on the other side of the ledger of which I only became aware much later. Predominant among these latter were the Liberals' charitable and social activities. They seemed to be in the front line in their endeavour to look after the stray sheep of Jewry. Their youth clubs were seemingly superior to those of the United Synagogue—the union of organized Traditional Jewry in Great Britain—and they displayed, too, a wonderful humanity in their public work for non-attached Jews.

I have often observed that those who are not religiously inclined are apt to accuse religious people of being indifferent, or even callous, to the needs of their brethren. Provided they can carry out their observances in comfort, say their detractors, they pursue their smug path of self-centred existence, undisturbed by the dangers threatening their fellows. And I must admit, quite frankly, writing now as an Orthodox Jew, that there is more than a modicum of truth in what the non-religious critics say. There is wonderful generosity among our people, but there is also a great deal too much stress on food, clothes, and luxurious holidays, while one sees often a sinful waste of money on such events as Barmitzvah and wedding celebrations—money which might better have been employed on advancing the cause of Judaism and its many urgent interests. A cultured people such as the Jews must, of course, have a relatively high standard of living, but too many seem determined to grasp with both hands every possible ounce of pleasure and luxury in this world, not ready to admit that there may be greater happiness in the next world.

It is, in my view, a most humiliating thought that so much of the work for the uplift and welfare of Jewish youth and others has been performed by the Liberals alone. If we could combine the good works of the latter with the genuine Judaism of the Orthodox we should indeed be a happy and powerful people. Perhaps the next generation of Orthodox Jews will not bury their heads in the sand. This is our only hope. Liberalism will some day die, as so many sporadic movements have died, but until Orthodox Judaism broadens its outlook upon humanity it can never exercise the influence which is so essential.

But at the period I am describing I thought, however erroneously, that what I listened to while sitting in Dr. Mattuck's congregation was Judaism, and I was bitterly disappointed. The sole satisfaction I derived from those sessions was that of being among Jewish people, for whom, as I have earlier related, I had felt so strong, though unexplained, an attraction even as a small boy.

I had always been very fascinated, too, by what I had seen of the peoples of India, and now, drawn to them afresh by their deeply religious nature, I felt bound to examine their claims. It chanced that there was among my acquaintances a most charming Indian student to whom I had been introduced by a young clergyman from Bombay, and from this friend, whom I will call Rana, I learned of many of the Hindu religious tenets.

This was not quite so simple as it sounds. Hinduism, it seemed to me as I listened, was simply a vast, all-sheltering umbrella beneath which countless millions of people, representing many different forms and shades of belief, found a spiritual home. Some of those forms I could only feel to be crude, vulgar, and utterly debasing. They appeared to symbolize sexuality run wild and to give little or no moral or spiritual uplift to their adherents. On the other hand, I realized, it was sheer stupidity for people who had experienced only one way of life, and that in a modern, sophisticated section of the world, to condemn offhand a situation which they did not even begin to understand. The teeming millions of India belonged to an existence beyond the vaguest conception of the average European; and while that average European was apt to regard the Indian as being backward at least in the matter of civilization, the Indian in turn looked down upon the white intruders in his country as pagans.

For the Indian could claim that he had at all events some form of philosophy or religion, whereas he was convinced that, apart from the missionary, whom he regarded as a mere pioneer of Imperialism, the majority of Europeans had nothing to worship save their own arrogance. That impression, Rana told me, was very widespread.

He explained to me, too, how an Indian is born into a certain caste, and that he could make no change in the caste status in which he found himself, and would not do so even if he could. He could, however, according to some shades of belief, undergo a change of caste, for better or for worse, in his next stage of reincarnation, depending upon his conduct in the current phase.

Rana seemed to think the system very practical and sensible; why struggle against the inevitable, he would ask. To my thinking, however, it all seemed very fatalistic, and I felt that to the millions of "untouchables" life must be incredibly hard. They had no privileges and no ambitions. As a tiny grain of sand in a vast desert, so was a man born into this unrecognized legion of humanity. The one saving grace was that possibility of a change for the better in a life to come, consequent upon the individual's behaviour here and now. I need scarcely add how glad it has made me to learn that nowadays, under Nehru's régime, the term "untouchable" has become taboo by law, that today the former outcasts are called by the infinitely more pleasing name "Children of God", and that still further reforms of their status are under way.

There seemed to me also, however, to be a very strong element of fear in Hinduism, involving a constant urge to placate the many angry gods and spirits who were ever close at hand to plague or injure. Such gross forms of the Hindu faith were apparently the only interpretation possible for the primitive minds of innumerable millions who constituted the lower strata of India's dense population.

Rana, being a high-caste Indian, was not a victim to the crude superstitions of his less-fortunate countrymen. His faith, in fact, was more a philosophy than a religion. There were certain laws of a dietary nature that he scrupulously observed, but his outlook was philosophical and universal. According to his ideas, the noblest sentiments in man were derived from the Infinite, who, it seemed, ruled the cosmos in a distant and disinterested sort of fashion.

I thoroughly enjoyed my discussions with Rana, and we became intimate friends. I had a profound respect and admiration for the mystic depth of his personality, and was much grieved when he was recalled to India to assist his father in the administration of his territories. I even determined that I would one day visit him in his land of charm and enchantment. But in spite of this deep personal attachment, I realized very clearly indeed that Hinduism could never satisfy my need for a revealed religion.

Not long after Rana's departure, it was my privilege to meet, at the League of Nations Union, a lady named Madame Favrat, who had been converted to Buddhism. She was an extremely well-educated woman and widely travelled. From her I learned the history of the faith she had embraced, and it was an eye-opener to me to discover that it claimed no less than one-third of the world's entire population. Any religion which held such sway was clearly worthy of investigation. Madame Favrat loaned me quite a small library of literature on the subject of Buddhism, and in addition to listening to her own most fascinating talks I attended lectures by Buddhist leaders.

Although Buddhism had originated in India, I learned, strange to relate it had not taken deep root there. It presented, in fact, a notable instance of the truism that a prophet is not accorded adequate honour in his own country. Buddha, whose infant name was Siddhartha, and who lived approximately five centuries before the time of Jesus, had been born a prince, and was therefore a person of quality in his own right. He entered this world, however, with a promise of greatness transcending by far the mere prestige of his royal lineage; for his mother, in a pre-natal dream, had seen a spirit descend into her from Heaven, and the message of this vision, as interpreted by the seers, was that a world ruler, or saviour, should be born to her.

In due course Siddhartha married a princess of surpassing beauty, but the happy, sheltered background to his life afforded him little satisfaction. He was sorely troubled by a problem which was disturbing the minds of many great prophets, philosophers, and other thinkers: namely, the transient nature of all things. His idealistic soul yearned for Nirvana—the condition of immutability. He felt this state of existence to be so desirable that no price which might enable him to gain it could be too heavy.

Accordingly, while still a young man in the prime of life, he turned his back upon his magnificent palace and riches, his beautiful wife and child, and went off to the lonely banks of a river, where he fasted almost to death. He soon came to regret having taken so extreme a course, however, and from then on he pursued a "middle of the road" ideal. He let it be known that he had been vouchsafed a revelation in which he was designated the Buddha, meaning the "Enlightened One", and commanded as such to go forth and spread the message through the world.

The essence of Buddha's teaching, as I understood it, was that all pain and sorrow spring from desire. It was precisely because we craved this, that, or the other that we experienced suffering. If only we could eliminate desire, peace would reign unchallenged in the heart and mind. And in prescribing this remedy for human ills Buddha had, I realized at once, fastened on to a very vital truth, one which had been preached by the thinkers of many religions, including the Christian mystics. Diogenes in his barrel, the Church's ascetics, and a multitude of others had realized that basic verity in their seeking to cut out the appetites of mind, body, and soul. Philosophy rightly thought that the happiest man is he who can live on least. The more props we need in life, the more difficult it is to travel. Even the great Dominican preacher of the 1930s, Bede Jarrett, in his admirable book, *No Abiding City*, reiterated in the clearest fashion the advantage of travelling light on our pilgrimage. Most people, he pointed out, needed far too much to get through life. Food, clothes, housing, the innumerable luxuries of modern life—all these weighed down their souls and hindered them from reaching the happiness which comes through detachment from earthly things. As I have said, I grasped the essential truth of such a doctrine; how far that attitude could be pursued in the rough and tumble of daily life, however, I did not feel so sure.

One aspect of Buddhism which, as explained to me,

appealed specially to my own form of idealism was its denial of a system of reward or punishment in the scheme of things. Buddha had contended that man should neither pray for particular objectives nor rebel against happenings which failed to accord with his desires. Every action would bring its own result. Goodness would result in goodness, evil in evil, as natural developments rather than as arbitrary rewards or penalties imposed from without by a sort of glorified schoolmaster on high. If a man lived a good life he would enjoy a better state hereafter—not as a prize, but as a natural outcome of his goodness.

Again, I could not but pay wholehearted tribute to Buddha's exhortation to his followers to love mankind with a perfect love. They should rejoice in another's joy, he insisted, and sorrow in another's grief. All this, of course, I recognized as inherent in all truly religious outlook; such premises as these lacked the crudity to be found in certain forms of Hinduism and, at the same time, avoided the dogmatic complications of Christianity. Had I not been so completely convinced that there must be somewhere a *revealed* religion which could satisfy all my demands, I might well have accepted the way of Buddha as a guide to life.

There was an aspect of Buddhism, however, with which I found it more difficult to sympathize: namely, the doctrine that there was no permanent soul in man. Everything, including the latter, was in a state of "becoming". Even God, according to Buddha, had no permanent identity. As a river flows into the ocean and becomes part of it, so did the soul of God, man, and everything in creation become absorbed into this eternal flux. Some people, not quite understanding the thought processes of Buddha, have accused his system of being atheistic. But it was not really that. Buddha, it is obvious, did believe in a supreme, or at least in a superior, Reality, which like Its inferiors, though in a different orbit, eternally "became" Something. The Greek philosophers, I need hardly add, were to develop this concept, which, correctly understood, had an undeniable basis of truth, inasmuch as change is an inevitable condition of growth.

So far as I was concerned, however, I did not, and could not, regard God as merely "becoming", but only as the totality of all "being", or rather, as Being Itself. God, I was convinced, was the Reality from whom all came, and unto whom all returned. Nor was He just a substantial lump of Being, as it were; He was the sum total of all life and perfection. He was distinct from His creation, not a part of it, as taught in Pantheism.

I felt that Buddhism, despite its recognition of the Godhead, presented a very vague and nebulous conception of it. It could not, in my eyes, qualify as a religion, at all events as a religion in the sense of what I sought. Its teaching impressed me deeply, but they could never add up to a *divinely revealed* religion. As I saw it, Buddhism was just yet another very beautiful and noble philosophy. It was not, I believed, a faith to live by. Philosophy could be most enlightening, interesting, and consoling, but it could not unite the creature to his Creator. It could enchant you in your study, but it could hardly help you along the road of life, or be meaningful to you when you had reached road's end.

Turning next to the study of Islam—my final effort for some considerable while—I accepted the invitation of a young student to accompany him to the Mosque at Woking, in Surrey. This student and I had become close friends. We frequently attended the Promenade concerts together, and from time to time we went away for a week-end by the sea. Like myself, he was of a religious inclination, and he likewise shared my doubts concerning our Anglican faith.

While at the university, my friend had met a girl from Cairo who had made rather a strong impression upon him, and so, apparently, her religious beliefs fascinated him. For some months the two of us discussed Islam; and although I failed to find in it the attractive features of either

Christianity or Buddhism, I was quite prepared to give it a fair chance.

Islam, although a truly amazing faith and imbued with a strong romantic flavour, struck me as harsh, restrictive, and placing far too much reliance on force. Its main attraction for me, I fancy, was the realization which gradually came to me that it, like Christianity, was a daughter faith of Judaism —the younger daughter.

Fascinating, too, was the story of the life and activities of Muhammed, to which I listened with the greatest care. That strange warrior-prophet had been born at Mecca in the year A.D. 570. His first realization of the rôle for which Providence destined him came when the sacred shrine of the Kaaba was rebuilt and he found himself chosen by lot to put the holy black rock in its place. Following retirement to a desert locality, he returned to his people convinced that he had been selected to lead them to righteousness. They being confirmed idolaters, Muhammed's task was an unenviable one, for idolaters and their idols are not easily separated.

Muhammed was firmly convinced, however, that there was but one God, and in the midst of his initial discouragement he received, like Elijah before him, a message of reassurance. He was not commanded to wash his garments and preach to the people. This injunction he very courageously obeyed forthwith, but his insistence that there was only the one God and no other brought upon him the fury of the populace. Had it not been for the sacred tradition that no blood could be shed in Mecca, he would doubtless have lost his life. Alas, there ensued a grievous relapse in Muhammed's spiritual life. For the time being he reconciled himself to idol-worship, and even falsely announced a vision of three goddesses who shared the divinity with Allah.

Eventually the Archangel Gabriel enlightened Muhammed, however, and from then on he never looked back. He preached the Unity of God without fear, and in A.D. 622 was forced to flee from Mecca to Medina in consequence. This date, that of the Hegira or Flight of Muhammed, marks the beginning of the Islamic Era. The Prophet was deeply disappointed, though, that the Medina Jews failed to embrace his revelation. Up till then he had enjoyed a favourable relationship with them and had even adopted the Jewish Sabbath. This he now changed to Friday in the new faith. Prayers were no longer recited facing towards Jerusalem, and the great Fast of the Atonement was replaced by that of Ramadan. Muhammed did, however, retain circumcision and forbid the consumption of pork.

Listening to the history of this religion, I found myself unable to help regretting the waning of its influence in world affairs, largely due, I supposed, to its having lost the power of material force. A sophisticated world, I also surmised, possibly finds the simple doctrine of One God, without an enveloping mass of mysteries, too prosaic and rarified for its complex mentality. As for its future, it is impossible to prophesy. Very few Muslims are converted to Christianity; but the Jewish faith has much in common with Islam, and I have never been able to understand why these half-brothers should continue in endless strife. In Israel the two live together in harmony, with Arab representatives holding seats in Parliament. A reunion between Jew and Arab would make a rich contribution towards the solution of world problems, whether political, moral, or religious. But Egypt, the self-proclaimed leader of the Arab world, is, of course, an implacable enemy of Israel.

For my part, I found in Islam too much this-worldliness, just as I was finding Christianity too other-worldly. And again, I found it hard to approve of the great prominence given to Muhammed himself in the Islamic outlook. The Prophet of Islam, although not worshipped as Jesus is by Christians, occupies a place among Muslims which Judaism allows to no man—not even to a prophet, Moses received the

Law itself on Sinai, yet we have no idea where his remains were laid, nor is any pilgrimage made by Jews to the place where he was last thought to have been. All honour has to go to the Creator; the prophet, no matter how great a prophet, was but His instrument.

3

No Peace of Spirit

"A hair perhaps divides the false and true."
Rubáiyát of Omar Khayyám, EDWARD FITZGERALD

"For with more wisdom is more worry. And increase of knowledge is increase of sorrow."
ECCLESIASTES, I, 18. (4)

THE non-Christian faiths having failed, in spite of their attractive philosophies, to satisfy my demanding needs, I felt that I must at least examine the claims of certain Christian groups outside the orbits of the major Churches.

I noticed, for instance, that the Christian Scientists were advertising their meetings very widely and renting the best halls and theatres. I read a large quantity of their literature and attended several of their gatherings. It struck me that most of those who frequented the meetings were of a prosperous class, dressed in expensive furs and arriving in luxurious cars. Scarcely ever did I see any working-class people in the audience.

The main point made by the various speakers was that sin and disease were merely states of mind. Pain was imaginary, evil simply a negation of reality. By adopting a right attitude of mind all manifestations of evil could be eliminated. You could, so to speak, "think" your toothache out of existence. Health and success were dependent upon proper thinking. Right thoughts radiated health, happiness, and prosperity. Mind over matter—that was the essence of the doctrine.

Mrs. Baker Eddy, the founder of this influential organization, had written, according to her lights, a "key" to the Scriptures. In this she explained the hidden mysteries of the life-giving Word. A *sine qua non* was harmony with the Heavenly Father, who, it seemed, stood to us likewise in a Mother-relationship. Jesus was portrayed primarily as a great healer, who, by inducing people to think correctly, cured them of their physical ills.

Whether cures claimed by the Christian Scientists were genuine or not I had no means of knowing. I found the teaching plausible but in no way convincing. One heard not infrequently of unnecessary deaths brought about by failure to call a doctor. I felt that for those who lived in very sheltered, peaceful surroundings it might well be possible to shut out the cruel realities of life. An expensive car, beautiful clothes, and a comfortable home might not remove all of a person's problems, but they indubitably could go a long way in that direction—and the majority of people in the congregation were, as I have said, of a social category to be able to enjoy such amenities.

I had to recognize, too, that the actual teaching of Christian Science held an element of truth. It was undeniable that the mind could influence the body to an almost incredible extent. Much of modern medical practice, in fact, was psychiatric. We lived in an age of neuroses, and a great deal of "illness" was in reality sickness of mind rather than of the body. Psychology, however, was still the infant of the sciences. Concerning the greatest wonder in the universe, the mind of man, we as yet knew relatively little.

Nevertheless, I felt a conviction that Christian Science took far too much for granted. It could not explain away either malignant growths, evil natures in men and women, or natural disasters. True, other faiths might not be able to offer an explanation of such things, but they did at least accept them as existing mysteries of life. Like Roman Catholicism, Christian Science attempted to give finite answers to too many problems that were *in*finite.

Moreover, Christian Science could lay claim to no real revelation. Prior to the advent of Mrs. Baker Eddy it had never been heard of; and excellent as the worthy lady's intentions might have been, she could show no identity card from Heaven. Jesus, Buddha, Muhammed—all of these had at least claimed some form of divine revelation; but Mrs. Eddy, one felt, was too close in time to our prosaic age to be accorded the status of even a minor prophet. In short, one could not exclude a strong suspicion of chicanery.

I therefore left the Christian Scientists to their smug complacency and continued my search among the miscellaneous splinter-groups of Christian profession. It led me next, during one of my visits to London, to the large and impressive building in the Euston Road which houses the Society of Friends, more familiarly termed the Quakers. Reading an announcement of their services, I decided to attend one Sunday evening.

Strictly speaking, a Quaker service is not supposed to be formal; the worshippers are expected to sit and wait until the Spirit moves them to speak, whereupon they should get up and deliver the fruits of their communings with Truth itself. This tradition appears, however, to have weakened in recent generations. On the occasion when I attended the Quaker service there was a set form of procedure. Two Friends supplied instrumental music and a third delivered an address on a prepared subject.

The meeting was none the less one which imparted an atmosphere of peace and sincere devotion. The Friends themselves were most charming people, giving the impression of being steeped in the spiritual life. From my conversations with them I learned much concerning the Society. As is generally known, the Quakers are uncompromisingly opposed to war, or indeed to any form of violence, though during the two world wars they rendered sterling service in ambulance units. They weighed their words with the utmost care, I observed, and lived in mortal fear of giving utterance to an untruth. Their ethics in business are of an amazingly high standard, and big English industrial families, such as the chocolate-manufacturing Frys, the Cadburys, and the Rowntrees, set a magnificent example to the business world of how to treat both their customers and their employees. I have nothing but admiration, in fact, for the Quakers as individuals and as a moral group. Yet even these good people could not give me the *revealed* form of faith for which I was still in search.

My experiences with the Spiritualist Church—if one may so call it—were brief and hardly congenial. I freely confessed, and still do, to a strong natural dislike for their creed and way of life. Call it prejudice if you like, but I had a distaste and even contempt for secret organizations. Furthermore, Spiritualism, in the sense of communing with the departed, was clearly condemned in Scripture. The only plausible case to be made for it, I felt, was that it endeavoured exclusively to contact good spirits and not evil influences from the other world.

The method of communication at the séance which I attended was through a medium, who claimed the distinction of being "psychic", or receptive to the influences of the spirit world. Having created the appropriate atmosphere, the gathering awaited signs of the approach of the spirit solicited. Those signs might be either external or simply subjective to the medium. The latter having fallen into a trance, a message was usually announced to have been transmitted to the person concerned, though sometimes the announcement was "number engaged" or words to that effect.

For myself, I declined to take any part in the proceedings, but the reaction of some of those attending the séance amazed me. Either they were dangerously clever actors or they really had received messages which shook them to their foundations. Some of those present with whom I spoke later claimed to have seen the astral bodies of former friends or relatives made manifest at meetings.

Unfortunately, in my view, the fact that such men of eminence as Sir Arthur Conan Doyle, Sir Oliver Lodge, and others supported Spiritualism gave it an air of respectability. The number of frauds perpetrated through the operation of mediums was a crying scandal. Widows, as a result of their confusion and mental distress, not infrequently parted with their savings and subsequently committed suicide.

While admitting the existence of such abuses, however, I have to add that it seemed to me there was evidence of real communication with the departed being a possibility. After all, the Bible tells us that saints received messages in visions by night, and many of the great events of religious history purport to have had a mystical background. But it also appeared quite evident to me, on the other hand, that when Providence wished to convey messages to living persons It did so unsolicited. Holy Writ and the most reliable religious guides were united in condemning the deliberate searching out of spirits with a view to ascertaining from them the things which God, in His wisdom and mercy, had hidden from human eyes.

And supposing, I asked myself, a person were to discover, through meddling with Spiritualism, that he was destined to die of, say, cancer within a specified period of time, would that serve any good purpose? Too many people, having consulted mediums about their future, had taken their lives rather than face their Destiny courageously.

I want to emphasize, however, that my doubts and qualms were entirely confined to the matter of Spiritualist trafficking in the unseen. I had no reason to question the existence of a future life; indeed, I sincerely believed in it and still do. Nor had I reason to doubt that Providence does sometimes use supernatural means of communication in Its dealings with men, and on two occasions in later years I had strange experiences which did nothing to lessen my belief in such possibilities.

One night at college I dreamed that a fellow student appeared before me, uttered the words "I have been expelled", and vanished. I had had little to do with the youth in question and knew nothing of his private life. So vivid had the dream been in every detail, however, that it made a very strong impact upon me—so much so that I could hardly take my eyes off him at breakfast next morning. And ten days later he *was* expelled. . . .

The other experience occurred at a time when I had been placed in charge of a certain young pupil, an orphan, who had just joined the college. Noticing that the boy was frequently very preoccupied and downcast, I suggested to him that he confide in me. For a long time he refused, but one afternoon, as we took a long walk together, he broke down and came out with it. He had, it seemed, made the acquaintance of a wealthy business-man from New York who had used him for the vile purpose of satisfying an unnatural lust. The boy had with him at the college a bundle of letters which at last, after much natural reluctance, he showed to me. They were the filthiest, most corrupting letters ever written, and were accompanied by a number of vilely obscene pictures. I urged him to take the bundle to the Rector. This he did, with the result that the wretched man was prosecuted and sent to prison on his next visit to England.

Not long afterwards, in the middle of one night, the boy became aware—or dreamed that he became aware, if you prefer it—of a menacing black figure standing over his bed. The ugly form bent over him, and seizing him in an iron grip, shook him almost to death. He woke in a flood of perspiration which had soaked his pyjamas and even the bedding, and for several days he was on the sick list.

Needless to say, I do not present this incident as having necessarily had any supernatural significance, but neither did I dismiss it as trivial, for the physical effects were too severe. Possibly it was just a particularly horrible nightmare, due to the poor boy dwelling so persistently on his degrading experience. But taking into consideration that he had never before had such a visitation, and so far as I am aware never had another, it was an impressive episode; and, as I have said, it in no way diminished my belief in the possibility of supernatural communications. So far as Spiritualism is concerned, however, my brief acquaintance with its procedures sufficed to convince me once and for all that this was in no sense of the word a faith by which I could live, and I then and there determined to have nothing more to do with it.

I mentioned earlier how I had decided to leave investigation of the Roman Catholic doctrines to a later date; but now, after my abortive attempts to find an answer to my inner needs from any of the other religious systems, I felt that the time had come to make a closer inquiry. It was at about this time that I noticed a huge sign outside a Catholic church in the neighbourhood of my home. It proclaimed a great mission by the Redemptorist Fathers, and the subjects advertised dealt precisely with those matters which were most disturbing me—"Is there a true Church?", "The Real Presence", and so forth. My ties with the Church of England had now become so loose that to all intents and purposes they no longer existed. I still looked back with gratitude to those Anglican guides of my early days, but that was not enough. I needed to know where I stood. My soul was torn apart. I simply had to find rest and peace of spirit. And so, although I felt far from comfortable at the idea of attending a Catholic service, I determined now to hear what Rome had to say. After all, I argued, great men in various walks of life were embracing the religion, so clearly there must be something in it. . . .

I would, I decided, attend the complete course of sermons, extending over a period of two weeks. On the following Sunday, therefore, I entered this Catholic church which, as was to be expected, I found filled to capacity. I became conscious at once of an overpowering atmosphere which I can only describe as hypnotic.

When the Redemptorist Father entered the pulpit, wearing a manifest air of assurance, he was able quite truthfully to claim that over 300,000,000 people all over the world implicitly believed what he himself believed. This was a powerful and plausible argument for a start, and it was precisely what I wanted to hear. Here at last was real authority deserving of serious thought. Was it not a species of miracle that so many people, representing so many very different nationalities and loyalties, should unquestioningly accept one and the same authority?

As the two weeks went by, the arguments of the Mission Fathers seemed to me more and ever more conclusive. A question, for instance, which had distressed me extremely up till that time had been that of the Real Presence of Jesus in the wafers and wine of Holy Communion. Here, however, the preacher took the sixth chapter of St. John's Gospel and showed quite clearly that if Jesus had spoken the words there recorded, then the bread and wine must of necessity change at the moment of consecration into the Body and Blood of Christ. The final stage of his argument removed my last lingering doubt. "Except ye eat the flesh of the Son of Man and drink His blood, ye have no life in you."

Dealing with the reaction of Jesus' listeners, the preacher made reference to their disbelieving attitude. Their answer had been, "This is a hard saying; who can receive it?" and they had begun to drift away. And Jesus, instead of turning to them and explaining away His words, had said to His very apostles, "Will you also go away?" The preacher took occasion to remark that the Protestants, unlike Jesus, did attempt to explain away those words. But thinking back on the sermon later on, away from that hypnotic atmosphere, it occurred to me that it had not stressed with the same emphasis the subsequent utterance of Christ in which He explained that His words were "spirit and life".

Despite such evasions, however, I badly wanted to believe. I was convinced that the Catholic Church had given me sufficient reason for believing, and my will was bent in that direction accordingly. Like so many incipient converts to Rome before and since, I felt that I could not spend the rest of my life looking for Truth. I had to have an anchor, and that soon. Everything in the Catholic Church, I perceived, was eloquent of security. It amounted to a spiritual insurance policy. Sign on the dotted line, and the Church, like a sort of spiritual Thomas Cook & Son, would see you and your luggage of cares and responsibilities safely into the Happy Land. Just stop thinking and cast all your problems into the vast, infallible machine which would resolve them all!

I knew later that when a convert is in that state no reasoning on earth is of any avail. "The Roman Fever", as it was once unkindly termed, is almost incurable. A few may recover, but hardly ever is a quick therapy effected. The convert must go through many personal experiences before he can be disillusioned by reason. When a person becomes a drug addict he finds it almost impossible to break free, and the few who do, suffer terribly in the process. So, too, is it with the few who discover their mistake in submitting to Rome and attempt to break loose. They go through hell before eventually they rediscover themselves and regain their complete freedom of spiritual life.

Like most people when they first experience the attraction of Rome, I was in a state of great emotional stress and strain. Youths in their 'teens and old men in their seventies are ideal potential material for conversion. The young man is searching for authority and the old man wants security, especially in face of approaching eternity. Great intellectual capacity can go hand in hand with spiritual poverty or, at all events, uncertainty. It can happen that a brilliant scientist or philosopher will, during a time of religious crisis, abandon all of his critical faculties and surrender everything to an authority which relieves him of the struggle. In his laboratory or study he questions everything, but when in church he assumes the diametrically opposite attitude.

And so it now was with me. Although on a far more modest plane, I had fully exercised my mind and carried out painstaking research into the complex subject of comparative religion. Yet here and now I felt unable, or at least unwilling, to struggle further. I had been presented with an adequate reason for unloading my burdens. The Catholic

Church seemed able to produce such excellent credentials. The logic, once you accepted certain premises, was flawless. So much so, in fact, that unless you did accept those fundamentals you felt it would be difficult to hold on to Christianity itself.

The service of Benediction, which followed the sermon, stirred me to my depths. The Celebrant, a majestic figure in his rich vestments, raised aloft the golden monstance in which was contained the sacred specie normally reserved in the tabernacle. As the hushed congregation bent low the priest moved the object of adoration over their heads, while the bell rang out dramatically through the silence in the big church. Celebrant and congregation then chanted the divine praises aloud in unison. The atmosphere was charged with a deep emotion. A soul in search of comfort and inspiration could not fail to be profoundly moved. . . .

At the end of the service I approached a priest and asked to be given a course of instruction in Catholicism. As the result of this, I placed myself in due course in the hands of a Jesuit, a man of great learning and piety who had himself been converted to Catholicism while a student at Oxford University. The tuition was lucid, cut-and-dried, and involved no practical difficulties—very different, in fact, from what I was later to encounter in Judaism.

The one stiff hurdle I had to surmount lay in accepting the Church's teaching on Eternal Punishment. This dogma the good Father tried to make easier for me by explaining that the only type of person who would really go to Hell would be the extreme sinner who practically set himself up as a hater of God. But not all Catholic theologians, he hastened to add, would feel able to entertain this interpretation of the doctrine of Eternal Punishment, and he suggested we shelve the problem for the time being. I agreed to shelve it. Another item in Catholic theology which worried me to some extent was the position of Mary. However, I made a colossal act of faith and swallowed this without argument. In fact,

I drank down the whole of the Church's consoling medicine, bottle and all. No more worry, no more strain. . . .

I even paid a visit to Lourdes and helped in ministering to the sick and infirm. There, too, the magic of this new fairyland worked its hynoptic charm, and I realized more and more clearly how carefully the Roman Church looks after its converts, and how completely foolproof is the system whereby they are conveyed from one stage of their journey to the next. A through ticket to the gates of Paradise is issued; and provided you do not lose your ticket, stamped "Faith", then through the gates you'll safely go. The pilot is infallible, the machinery guaranteed against any possibility of breakdown. No wonder Rome can count 10,000 converts in Britain alone each year. Nobody, however, knows for certain what is her rate of leakage, though considered opinion holds that she loses as many as she gains. But she does at least know approximately how she stands, and her organization is nothing short of superb. Even non-Catholic powers consider it worth their while to maintain a representative at the Vatican. It is the ears and eyes of the world.

In my new *milieu* I found peace, for the time being at all events, and the day came at last when I was invited to offer myself for the work of souls—that dedication of my life's labours which I had so ardently desired when I was a schoolboy. It was at this point that I received the news of the death, from cancer, of my childhood guardian, Mrs. Jackman. It was a terrible blow. But I now had the strength to face this tragedy, for all doubts and uncertainties had at that time been thrust from my mind, all moral and spiritual cares cast upon the broad shoulders of Rome.

The tidings of Mrs. Jackman's death made me decide to accept the invitation to enter the priesthood, for now I was free to give my entire self to the work. Accordingly, it was arranged that I should be enrolled as a student at the Catholic College of Campion House, in Middlesex. This was in

1934, and I was to spend the next four years there in revising the Humanities and preparing for a subsequent study of Philosophy.

From the moment of my reception into the Roman Catholic Church I had started to make new, kind friends on all sides, who virtually eliminated any sensations of strangeness or loneliness I might otherwise have experienced. What a contrast to the chilly indifference with which, as I later discovered, the convert to Judaism is treated! The convert to the Catholic Church is welcomed and left in no doubt from the earliest moment that he is wanted and acknowledged as one of the flock. And so, from the very beginning, I found myself caught up in a round of charitable families who took me into their hearts and homes as though they had known me all their lives. In the midst of my sorrow at Mrs. Jackman's death and the consequent sense of no longer "belonging", this human warmth came to me as a new lease of life.

At Campion House I met many other converts drawn from various walks of life. Every moment of my four years there was enjoyable; the community life appealed to me, and the intellectual stature of my teachers was an inspiration. My classics master was another convert from Oxford, where he had been a distinguished don. And the entire staff, from the Rector down, were graduates of either Oxford or Cambridge. The Catholic Church, in her wisdom, gives only the best in education and living conditions to her students for the priesthood. This has a propaganda value, it is true, but it is also strictly in accord with the policy set by such cultured Popes as Pius XI and Pius XII. At the particular time of which I am writing, in fact, Pope Pius XI was urging most strongly upon the bishops of the Catholic world the advisability of weeding out any candidate who lacked the ability to complete the long course of studies in a satisfactory manner.

As time went on and I progressed in my studies, I came to appreciate more and more clearly how wide the gulf is between Roman and non-Roman Christianity. I do not like making definite statements concerning the future, but of one thing I am absolutely certain: there never will be a reunion between Rome and the other Churches. The nearest approach to a bridge—if indeed it can be called even that—has lain in the emergence and growth to power of the Church of England's Anglo-Catholic party. Anglo-Catholic churches differ little in many respects from those of the Roman communion. There are Mass (sometimes in Latin), Confession, and various other essentially Roman institutions. In one matter only do they never conform, but it is one of paramount importance: namely, the Papal authority, though there are, in point of fact, Anglo-Catholic churches which do offer up prayers for the Pope.

Were the Anglo-Catholic party to secede to Rome, I used to surmise, a very serious blow would be dealt to the Church of England. And yet this would, on the other hand, simplify what is at present a strange and anomalous situation. The wide variance between forms of worship, and consequently of belief, within the Established Church must prove a nasty headache for the Primates. According to strict interpretation of the law, as matters stand at present, many clergy could be proceeded against for illegal practices in worship. But a number of bishops turn a blind eye to the Anglo-Catholic parishes in their dioceses, quietly thanking God, no doubt, for a few centres of life and progress. Wherever the Evangelical Church has a specially strong character, as was the case in my own boyhood church, it can be filled. But the Anglo-Catholic churches are usually much better attended than those of the Low Church variety. In many parish churches with seating capacity for a thousand, only a hundred or so of worshippers keep up regular attendance, and often less.

So far as I could tell, however, Anglo-Catholic secession to Rome was something outside the bounds of possibility. Influential though the Anglo-Catholic party might be, it was in reality no more favourable to Rome than were the Broad

Church or the Low Church party. And as for Rome herself, she often preferred the out-and-out Protestant to the Anglo-Catholic, just as the Kremlin often prefers the dyed-in-the-wool, true-blue Conservative to the Socialist.

What, then, I speculated, could be the ultimate outcome of this sharp division between the Roman and non-Roman Churches? Either, I concluded, the non-Roman faiths would have to submit to Rome, which was clearly out of the question, or Christendom would continue split in two until the end of time, with the "balance of power" maintained. For actually, if one included the Greek and Russian Orthodox Churches, there were as many non-Roman Christians in the world as Roman Catholics. So presumably Protestantism would remain hopelessly weakened by its divisions and controversies, and totally lacking in real leadership, authority, and discipline, while Catholicism, for its part, would go on filling its churches with people content to leave the welfare of their souls to the Vatican's infallible judgment. All they needed to do was to adhere strictly to the splendid discipline laid down for the regulation of their spiritual life. If you missed Mass you were in mortal sin. Why go to Hell and burn in everlasting fire when half an hour in church once a week was the simple solution?

Following my four years at Campion House, I passed on to St. Mary's College, Birmingham, to study philosophy. Here, again, I found a deep satisfaction in the teachings of the great minds of the past. At this stage the mysteries of religion were not in the forefront of one's thinking, and the professors were men of deep piety and profound learning. The atmosphere was spiritually and intellectually satisfying to me from every point of view, and I was sorry when the time came for me to leave the pleasantly scholastic life of St. Mary's and progress to yet another institution, the Pontifical Bede College. This college is situated at Rome in normal times, but because of the War, it had been evacuated to Upholland College, in Lancashire, England, "for the duration"—and here I was to apply myself to the study of Dogmatic Theology.

As can be gathered from certain of my observations in the preceding paragraphs, even during my stay at Campion House my thinking had not invariably been of a strictly orthodox variety. But there and at St. Mary's my particles of doubt had been temporarily stilled in my enjoyment of the pleasant community atmosphere. It was now, at the Pontifical Bede College, that those incipient misgivings began gradually but inexorably to return.

4

Autocracy in the Clergy

"Tyranny is a habit capable of being developed, and at last becomes a disease. The man and the citizen disappear forever in the tyrant."

DOSTOYEVSKY

"Ben Zoma said: Who is mighty? He, who subdues his passions, as it is said: (Proverbs 16, 32) 'He that is slow to anger is better than the mighty, and he that ruleth over his spirit than he that takes a city' ".

MISHNA—Sayings of the Fathers 4.1 (5)

A THEOLOGICAL seminary is an eminently peaceful place in which to live. The regularity of the life, with its division of activity between the sacred and the secular, creates a sense of security which people in the world outside rarely, if ever, enjoy. I was particularly attached to the Vice-Rector, a young theologian of outstanding gifts and brilliant intellect. He took Cardinal Newman as his guide in all things, and despite a dreamy manner and a tendency to lapse into prose in his lectures, he commanded universal veneration from the students, who were conscious of the sincerely spiritual texture of his life and teaching.

In spite of the congenial atmosphere of the Pontifical Bede College, however, it was at this stage that doubts began to re-enter my mind with new force. I was slowly but surely freeing my thinking from that "hypnosis" of the critical faculties which overcomes the neophyte in Catholicism. I allowed myself to read more widely than the authorities would have sanctioned had they known; and the more I read, the more deep-seated and the more distressing did my doubts become.

To be specific, I was commencing to feel that Christianity, much as I still respected it in many regards, offended my understanding of Almighty God. It seemed to me quite unworthy to present the Ruler of the Universe as a baby born of an earthly mother, and the fact that He was supposed to have no father on earth appeared only to render the doctrine that much the more reprehensible. Furthermore, the idea of three persons in the Godhead was, to my thinking, a gratuitous assumption and one which detracted from, rather than enhanced, the glory of God, since it struck directly at the basic conception of God's unity.

Then there was that doctrine of Eternal Punishment, which I could only consider a gross caricature of the nature of the God of Mercy. Indeed, it was difficult to understand how it was possible for those who accepted such a monstrous dogma to criticize Judaism as negative and harsh; and even Purgatory, the intermediate state in which souls worked off a debt of punishment in respect of sins already forgiven, struck me as being likewise a form of calumny against the character of the Eternal Father of mankind.

I simply could not, in my then mood of disaffection, believe that the notion of a supremely kind and good God committing a sinful soul to unending torment should find a place in any enlightened heart. And conversely, the whole business of spiritual trading, as exemplified in the system of indulgences and intercessary mediums, seemed to me to turn Heaven into a glorified market-place. I felt sure a time must eventually come when the educated masses would throw off this crudely commercial religion, with its dispensations and back-door permissions to escape the consequences of one's personal actions.

Nor could I unquestioningly accept the Sacramental system whereby men indirectly partook of supernatural life. I saw it as artificial and of human design rather than as of divine revelation. Although millions of perfectly worthy people sincerely believed that the Communion they received was the actual body and blood of Jesus, there seemed no adequate reason for assuming such a fantastic transmutation. That God should lie concealed within the species of bread and wine presented, to my thinking, a situation beyond all credibility. To entertain such a notion seemed to be an offence to the majesty of God and something dangerously akin to idolatry. I stigmatized it as being "theophagy" rather than theology.

The Church of Rome, of course, in its skilful and elaborate

propaganda, plays down these perplexing teachings. But the fact remains that nobody can call himself a Catholic unless he, ostensibly at all events, accepts them without question. I find it difficult to decide what alteration might have come about in the course of my life had I continued to give full rein to my misgivings. But a change of occupation and environment in the summer vacation of 1942, when I worked with a sense of temporary emancipation and much enjoyment under Lord Woolton at the Ministry of Food on tasks which required considerable concentration, brought of necessity a break in my tormenting self-communings; and on my return to college I resolutely threw my doubts behind me and gave myself wholly to the preparations for my entry into the active labours of priesthood.

The day of my ordination by Archbishop McDonald in St. Mary's Cathedral, Edinburgh, was a red-letter day in more senses than one, for Mussolini had fallen from power the previous night. In due course I found myself robing for the ceremony, and then, as the procession formed, the organ pealed out in the "War-march of the Priests" from "*Aida*", and there I was, in company with my fellow deacons, solemnly preceding the Archbishop to the altar. Prostrate on the ground, I had conferred upon me the full powers of the priesthood, transmitted from the Apostles down through the ages for nineteen centuries. From henceforth I was empowered to celebrate the mysteries of the Catholic Church, to preach, to hear confessions, and to console the faithful in all their afflictions.

The cathedral was packed to capacity with a congregation which included Protestants as well as Catholics. At the close of the ceremony hundreds lined up in queues to receive my blessing at the altar rails, and among them were actually two Protestant ministers. At a luncheon which followed a second ceremony, at the Jesuit Church in London, I entertained a large company which included Mrs. John Winant, the wife of the United States Ambassador. Mr. Winant himself was to have been there also, but was unavoidably detained at the Embassy.

The whole affair had been one tremendous thrill from beginning to end. Little did I realize on that great day that within seven years the magnificence would have crashed in ruins about me.

Could I have had my wish, I would have remained in a college atmosphere after my reception into the priesthood, continuing a life of study, prayer, meditation, and teaching. It was soon made clear to me, however, that this was not to be my portion. From the short-lived glory of my ordination ceremony I arrived at my first parish, that of Dalkeith, just outside Edinburgh in Scotland, where I threw myself with vigour into the parochial work. I got on well with the parish priest, who, although he bore a certain facial resemblance to Mussolini and at times acted in a manner reminiscent of that recently fallen despot, was a thoroughly good pastor of souls.

It was not long before Monsignor McGettingan, the Vicar-General, who was also Administrator of the cathedral, was kind enough to invite me to deputize for some of his own clergy who were away on holiday. This was a wonderful opportunity for me to win my spurs, so to speak, and I seized it with both hands. The congregations were always tremendous, seldom less than a thousand. And with all due modesty I could not disguise it from myself that I possessed a real flair for preaching. Indeed, I could sense from the very start that I was holding my listeners, and I was human enough to revel in the realization of it.

However, as I have said, my activities were not confined to preachings, but consisted for the most part in ordinary parish routine. Although I was to return to college for a post-ordination course, I worked as though I was permanently attached to the cathedral. Instead of merely preaching on Sundays and resting during the week, as I was entitled to do as a student priest, I climbed the stairs of dirty tenements in search of lost youths and took part in organizations for their welfare. In point of fact, the Administrator was anxious to have me posted to the cathedral, but the Archbishop was adamant in his refusal to permit it.

Within the cathedral itself Monsignor McGettingan ruled supreme. He was a saint and a scholar, one whom I could revere without reservation. Deprived by a totalitarian prelate of his proper function of helping to govern the Archdiocese, McGettingan had thrown all his genius into the adornment of the cathedral and the maintenance of its magnificent liturgy. The music was nothing short of superb. The High Mass on Sundays was a wonderful combination of dignity, artistic splendour, and choral perfection. To experience it was a happy introduction to what I fondly hoped would be a very promising ministry.

So long as there was implicit obedience to his dictates, the Archbishop allowed the Administrator a free hand in these matters. But upon that implicit obedience he insisted. Just now I termed him a "totalitarian prelate", and truly that was no exaggeration. Archbishop McDonald, O.S.B., of St. Andrew's and Edinburgh, had for years been the Abbot of a huge monastery, and there were many who felt that he regarded his secular clergy as monks at large. His stress on minute obedience was certainly characteristic of a monastic prince rather than of a Chief Shepherd of souls. In his view there was but one way to look, think, or act: namely, precisely as His Grace looked, thought, or acted. Heaven help the independent or individualistic thinker! The crozier would crack his skull in double quick time.

It is only rarely that the Holy See has appointed an abbot to rule an archdiocese, for experience has not favoured the experiment. Monks are usually men admirable enough in the environment of their religious establishments, but when set in authority over parish clergy they are apt to display a complete lack of understanding. And so strenuously have the parish clergy objected to such appointments in consequence, that few have been made in recent years. There have, of course, been one or two notable exceptions to this general unsuitability of abbots for diocesan authority, but they have only served to point the rule, and Archbishop McDonald was not of their number.

The Archbishop has long since gone to his rest, and "Of the dead speak nothing but good" is a fine maxim, though I have heard it flippantly misquoted as *De mortuis nil nisi bunkum.* Be that how it may, I shall not be contravening that maxim when I say that Archbishop McDonald seemed like some medieval prelate who had somehow stepped into the twentieth century out of a stained-glass window. Such men, while not belonging to our age, do at least give it impetus and colour.

I well remember the shock I experienced on ringing up Archbishop's House as a new student. I asked for the secretary, and I all but dropped the receiver when His Grace answered the telephone in person. I was swept into the presence and hardly had time to realize what had happened before the interview was over. But my personal relationship with him thereafter was excellent. I was, in fact, his "blue-eyed boy" until the time when, as I shall relate in its proper place, I ran foul of his dictatorial attitude.

His Grace lived a Spartan life, permitting himself no sort of luxuries in spite of the comfortable circumstances of his family, who were whisky-distillers. He slept on an iron cot and rose almost at dawn each morning to pray. Letters were frequently answered in his own illegible scrawl, and the stamps were invariably stuck on upside down. Malicious rumour had it that this last-named foible was a remnant of his Jacobite leanings, though beyond question he was loyal to the Crown. He could be amazingly generous, yet on frequent occasions he showed himself mercilessly harsh. He was a giant in every respect—sometimes too much of a giant, in fact, for well-meaning but errant curates. The one verse in Scripture which appeared to have escaped him was that which refers to the "smoking flax and the broken reed". If he just once drew his sword, or rather raised his crozier, the transgressor might just as well pack his bag, for life from that moment on was sheer hell.

Like most authorities who in the exercise of their power discard constitutional tradition, the Archbishop was at the mercy of tale-bearers. Men actuated by jealousy or plain malice could drop poison into the archiepiscopal ear, and forthwith some perfectly innocent person would be damned out of hand. An Archbishop usually allows himself to be guided by his Chapter of Canons, but His Grace's canons might just as well have lived in Timbuctoo, and I daresay they often wished they had! His Vicar-General was in a perpetual state of siege, so to speak, and spent most of his time either decorating the cathedral or discussing the latest issue of *The Tablet.* He and the Archbishop would, if I may be permitted so irreverent a simile, bare their teeth and spit at each other in the vestry like a pair of belligerent cats.

In point of fact, the diocese was virtually ruled by a committee of clergy who usurped the rightful functions of the canons. One of them was barely out of his long clothes, and it must have been nauseating in the extreme to experienced members of the Venerable Chapter to find themselves ousted by clerical saplings. There is something to be said for bureaucracy; but there is far more to be said for traditional government carried on by experienced and well-balanced men. The flashes of genius may be fewer, but so are the flashes in the pan and miscarriages of justice.

His Grace used to boast that his ancestors had been cattle-lifters, and certainly he could have held his own in any skirmish, though in these modern days his skirmishing could be only of the verbal sort. He delighted in uttering tirades against the Soviet, proving himself in that respect wiser than his generation. He was full of admiration for England for her part in saving Europe, but voiced constant warnings against the dangers of Communism, and had he been alive today the Press assuredly would be carrying banner headlines over scathing references by His Grace to Messrs. Khruschev and Company. He almost got himself involved in a court case with Sir Hartley Shawcross, an encounter in which the majority of people seemed to think he came off best. The Archbishop was a zealot of the type that would have delighted in a sojourn in gaol for the sake of his convictions. He called a spade a spade, and sometimes even a purple shovel!

Had Archbishop McDonald dwelt a little more apart and worked through constitutional channels, I think he might have avoided many grave errors. But then, of course, it would not have been His Grace. We have to pay a price for great men; perhaps they are a luxury. Certainly the mediocre instrument leaves more room for divine operation. The Archbishop died as he had lived, swiftly and without fuss. Gazing upon the earthly remains of this courageous but impetuous ruler, I felt an overpowering sense of tragedy—the tragedy of departed glory. The despot who had sent so many from his presence in abject trepidation now lay powerless.

To return, however, to my experiences in the field of parochial duties. I often marvelled, in later years, how on earth I had managed to get through all the work I did get through each week. In addition to my youth work, I regularly visited the sick and looked up the lax. But that was not all by a long chalk. Near the parish there was a "Bevin Boys' Hostel", one of the establishments set up during the War to house those boys over a certain age and not yet in uniform whom Ernest Bevin, as Minister of Labour, had recruited to work in the coal-mines. Coal was a first priority in national needs, and these lads held a place of supreme importance in our fight for survival.

The Bevin Boys, who were trained at centres established near the pit-heads, came from every type of home and included rich and poor, educated and illiterate. But the scheme brought them all together under one roof. A further complication lay in the fact that these lads worked side by side with the veteran miners. It was amazing how well the plan worked, though it has to be recollected, of course, that the British Empire had its back to the wall, and that Ernest Bevin was an outstandingly strong character. In normal times, I am sure, boys of such widely different backgrounds could have been welded together only with the utmost difficulty.

The local mine manager invited me to take an interest in the Bevin Boys under his care, and of course I agreed. I visited the hostel, talked with the youths, and organized social functions. To my understandable gratification, the great majority of them responded; in fact, I felt that my effort was one of the most rewarding of all my social-welfare ventures. Within a week of my being asked to help, a committee of the boys had been formed and a programme of activities drawn up. And what was more, I insisted upon including boys representing faiths outside of my own denomination, though this, I regret to add, was done in the face of the strongest objections on the part of the ecclesiastical authorities.

In due course I had the opportunity to go down the coal-mine, and it was a revelation to me to see the cool courage with which the miners worked. We are apt to forget the extremely dangerous conditions under which those who obtain our coal fuel live and labour. No matter how careful the management may be, the margin of danger in the life of every miner is much wider than that of almost any other calling. When we criticize their claims for a higher standard of living and a greater measure of economic security for themselves and their dependants, we should meditate deeply upon the hazards to which they are hourly exposed. One false move or a thoughtless stroke of the pick, or for that matter a piece of mere bad luck, will involve them and their comrades in serious injury and possible death.

The grumblers should spend, as I spent, a couple of hours in a damp, dangerous pit; it would surely serve to revise their opinions. I watched the miners, stooping low and working in pools of water, with only the light of their lamps to assist them, extract the precious commodity at the risk of their very lives. Every time a miner goes down to the coal-face he is taking his life in his hands. His wife and children can never be sure of seeing him return alive.

When tragedy does strike, it is, of course, a priest's bounden duty to go down the pit in order to administer what spiritual comfort he can to the injured and the dying. I well remember once being summoned to the pit-head after a major disaster had occurred. I insisted on being allowed to descend the shaft; and in spite of violent protest on the part of the management, who stressed their inability to undertake any form of responsibility for my safety, I went down to see what could be done.

On reaching the foot of the shaft, I had to wait for some considerable time in semi-darkness, surrounded by an atmosphere which spoke tragically and most realistically of the presence of death. I could see in the distance dim lights approaching in that measured, funereal march which was to bring the victims for a conditional absolution and blessing. The survivors stood in a circle around the bodies of their friends, reciting prayers with the fervour and devotion of monks in a monastery. Having done all that could be done, I emerged into the welcoming daylight, but only to engage upon the even more difficulty duty of breaking the tragic news to relatives prostrated with grief.

The communicating of bad news to a wife and family is the most painful task of all for the priest. The miner's wife must ever dread the knock upon her door when her husband is at work, for the messenger can so easily be an angel of death. But those who minister to the spiritual and moral needs of others must be prepared to witness a very large measure of sorrow. And no explanation is ever possible, nor do words of comfort usually seem at all adequate. A semi-silent sympathy is often the only formula.

One of my chief worries was parental apathy. I well remember a visit I paid to an Approved School administered by an Order of Brothers. The inmates were boys who had been accepted on probation following crimes of varying degrees of seriousness. Unhappily the proportion of juvenile delinquents in the Catholic community was rather above the average. This is no reflection upon Catholics as such, but rather upon the social handicaps under which they lived for such a length of time. As the standard of living among the working classes improved, this state of affairs mended likewise.

Talking with the boys at the Approved School, I was appalled at the shocking home conditions which many of them disclosed. Parents appeared altogether uninterested in, and often even criminally negligent of, their children's welfare. They could not account for their offspring's conduct for the very simple reason that most of the time they were not even aware of their children's whereabouts. While they sat drinking in public-houses, their children roamed the streets learning evil ways. Such mothers as were not drinking or sleeping with strange men were working in factories to obtain more money to spend on more selfish amusements. I seriously wondered whether it might not have been more just to send the parents for a strict course of training in care of the young than to condemn their sinfully neglected children to an institutional existence. The law, it seemed to me, was far too lenient with neglectful parents. More and more of the latter were casting their burdens upon the State. The teacher, the club leader, and the *clergyman* were being saddled with purely parental tasks which it was certainly no part of their duty to discharge.

I am glad to say, however, that there was occasionally a somewhat lighter side to my parochial work, even where the local backsliders were concerned. I remember an encounter I had in the course of my initial walk round the town after taking up my post in the parish. The first parishioner to greet was Paddy O'Roorke. It was a Saturday afternoon, and Paddy, after a three hours' session in the local public-house, was on his way home on two very unsteady legs to appease an angry wife with a bunch of flowers.

"Praise be to God, Father, and may ye be wid us for years to come!" was his salutation.

This hearty greeting cheered me. I saw that Paddy was a character, but it was mercifully hidden from me to what extent this was true. Most sinners are content with a choice of either drink, horses, or women. Paddy, however, was very greedy: he went all the way with all three. And the pity of it was that he had a model wife who kept his home beautifully clean, plus a brilliant son who spent all his leisure hours working hard for a degree in engineering. Paddy thought the world of this boy and boasted perpetually of his brains and industry. Another boy, the youngest, was both deformed and mentally afflicted, but Paddy adored him equally. In fact, he was immensely proud of his whole family. Unhappily the family could not find any source of pride in Paddy in return. On Christmas Eve he invited me to administer the pledge to him and bless his home. This I did, and for a week or so Paddy held out. But then, alas, his propensities regained the upper hand, and all his good resolves were abandoned.

Thus then my parochial duties were of light and shade, and the humorous and tragic were constantly interwoven.

5

Suspension—Now What?

"Pierced to the depth of my heart by a blow unforeseen—and mortal."

Le Cid, PIERRE CORNEILLE

"All the Divisions of Hell rule over the angry man."

THE TALMUD, Nedarim 22a. (6)

It was in my youth work that I had found true contentment; and in view of what ultimately came to pass I must re-emphasize the fact which was to prove in the end my undoing, or rather my salvation, as I prefer to consider it: namely, that in spite of all hierarchial frowns, I resolutely declined to exclude non-Catholics, whether Protestant or professing no faith at all, from my work of moral and spiritual rehabilitation.

While my work with the Bevin Boys had started so auspiciously, it was a matter of great regret to me when in due course I found myself transferred to another parish. The one to which I went next was in the large town of Stirling, with its rather interesting mixture of the ancient and modern with the historical and industrial.

And it was here, to my great delight, that I met for the first time with a very wonderful movement, the Young Christian Workers. This international youth organization was founded by a highly zealous Belgian pastor, who was the son of a poor workman. At the deathbed of his father, who lived and died in poverty, he had solemnly vowed that he would spend his life in raising the material, moral, and religious status of the young worker. There was a wide gap between the latter and the Church. He determined to bridge it. And he kept his vow, for he established study-groups for young boys from the factories, training them by the "See, Judge, and Act" method to improve their own lot and that of their fellow workers.

His study-groups absorbed the social teaching of Popes Leo XIII and Pius XI, applying the principles to the problems of the day. The threat of Communism was more apparent then, if not more real, than it is at present. The young worker was taught to overcome the tyranny of Communism with the sword of justice. The movement spread throughout the world, and was instrumental in bringing thousands of youthful workers back to the Catholic Church. There were certain very reactionary priests, it is true, who attempted to hinder and obstruct the efforts of the movement. The Church, however, fostered it wholeheartedly, and our own Archbishop, to his great credit, gave it every assistance.

It was a happy day for me, amid the trials and frustrations of my parochial work, when I was appointed Chaplain to the Young Christian Workers. The idea was that I should, in this capacity, remain behind the scenes, while the leaders of the movement themselves contacted the young workers, particularly the ones who had lapsed. They would, it was believed, gradually draw these into their meetings, and in due time thereafter they would be helped by the Chaplain.

I began to see in this movement the only instrument in existence, so far as I was aware, for closing the gap between modern youth and religion. But I have often since then reflected upon the wide discrepancy between Rome's official teaching through the movement and the poor social conditions existing, for example, in Spain and Italy, where the Church's social instruction seems to be observed more in the breach than in the performance. These may be happy enough lands, but in some of their provinces they are also extremely backward and very far from enjoying the social standards of the Welfare States. I found myself quite unable to comprehend the servile attitude of the Church in Spain towards General Franco and the seeming reluctance of other Catholic countries' churches to press forward with social reform. The ubiquity of mendicants in Catholic lands, to mention but one symptom, is depressing in the extreme.

The intense activity involved in this happy movement, the

Young Christian Workers, served to drown my resurgent doubts, at least for the time being. I knew so well that the everlasting problem of evil exercises the mind of youth, with its burning passion for justice, far more than most of us realize. And yet, paradoxically, the masses of 'teen-agers who gave all their leisure hours to dancing and other accepted forms of recreation had not the slightest interest in organized religion. Nevertheless, I felt I could understand their apathetic attitude. Why, after all, should they have regard for organized religion when so many professedly religious people showed themselves in reality so utterly unsympathetic and narrow-minded?

And I know that the irreligious youth of the day were suspended in mid-air, so to speak. Even for young people with a more or less religious background the ordinary youth clubs catered only in a very unimaginative fashion, and the youths with no such background at all were simply nobody's business. There were, needless to say, some wonderful exceptions to this general rule—men of the highest calibre, such as Sir Basil Henriques of London, Scotland's Major Crum, and various others, who sacrificed comfort and ambition to remain near to, and work for, unattached youth. These men really did perceive the problem and went out of their way to tackle it.

Sixty per cent of 'teen-agers—and the figures have changed little since then—had no religion, and the fault was not theirs. Religious and educational authorities were too often in a groove, hesitating to go forth to meet the young rebel of our century with a sympathetic heart and hand. As for the churches, the freer atmosphere in the Nonconformist places of worship seemed to me, on the frequent occasions when I visited them, to present a medium most likely to be attractive to youth. But the attendances were no longer what they had been. England appeared to be giving up organized religion and relying more and more upon radio and television for its spiritual food. The Roman community, and to a lesser extent the Jewish community, did, it was true, cater for religious training outside the home. But whereas in Judaism external instruction seemed less urgent because of its being the very centre of home life, in Christian circles the Sunday School seemed to be the alpha and omega of moral and spiritual moulding.

It is no exaggeration to say that this problem of the non-attached youth obsessed me. One day, I hoped and trusted, I might be able to do something really substantial towards its solution. In the present state of this world, alas, it looked as though those who had the vision had no money, while conversely those who possessed the money were devoid of vision —concerning the problems of the rising generation, at all events.

For a time all went well with me. But inevitably, despite the blessed sedative of my work with the Young Christian Workers, a day came when I had to recognize that my religious doubts, though temporarily lulled into quiescence under its distracting influence, had continued very strong underneath the surface. Year by year they had taken deeper root in my subconscious mind. It needed only a shock to bring them right back into active life; yet I felt at this stage that there might still be time for them to be dispelled if circumstances should come about to show me some new approach.

As matters were, however, I found my attention focusing upon a very different sort of vista, one which undoubtedly would have profoundly disturbed my superiors and colleagues had they gotten wind of it. Although my leisure hours were few and far between, I had managed to extend my reading on comparative religion, and the writings of Professor Klausner and other brilliant Jewish authors on the origins of Christianity were slowly but surely persuading me that Judaism, handed down to the children of Israel from Sinai, represented the truly ideal way of life. Christianity, I had come to believe, no matter how good and noble, could only be regarded as an offshoot of that ancient Mother Faith. . . .

My long-standing suspicion that Jesus was never really anything other than a practising Jew was gradually hardening into a positive conviction. It seemed obvious that St. Paul had been the founder of the Christian faith as it is known to us today. Faced with the problem presented by the Gentile mission-field, he had shrewdly decided to give Judaism a good admixture of Hellenism, thus providing the pagan world with an easy compromise.

Judaism in its pure form, Paul apparently realized, was much too rarefied for Gentile consumption. The notion of worshipping an unseen God was beyond the grasp of the nations. The idea, however, of an incarnate God who walked the earth out of love for mankind was much easier of acceptance, and the Greeks had already cherished just such a conception. Paul, being the practical and apostolic soul that he undoubtedly was, and realizing that Judaism *per se* could never appeal to masses so long accustomed to images and visible, tangible deities, had fused the two conceptions with brilliant results. The Church thus evolved was able to offer those masses all the most attractive features of their old religions, but modified by the notion of One God.

When celebrating the elaborate rites of the Catholic Church, I became increasingly aware of the marked similarities between the Roman liturgy and the old Temple services. Indeed, many of the prayers and ceremonies were almost identical. When, for example, the priest, during a sacred moment of the Mass, placed his hands, with thumbs turned downward, upon the chalice containing the consecrated wine, he was performing the very action of the Temple priest who held his hands in precisely the same posture over the scapegoat. The Easter ritual, too, abounded in Jewish ceremonial and even prayers. Over and over again, in fact, in the prayers of the Roman Church, direct links with the old religion of Jerusalem were manifest.

In short, the signs were clearly visible that I was turning my steps in the direction of the Synagogue, and the time had come when I had to face the fact. It can be more easily imagined than described what a deepening disgust, in these circumstances, I experienced in the performance of my priestly duties. I functioned under an oppressive sense of hypocrisy. My preaching, once self-evidently carrying such conviction, became formal and empty. My administration of the Sacraments was perfunctory.

The one salvation for me was the deep satisfaction I derived from my external work in the parish, and particularly so because it brought problems to be met and overcome. My new parish priest was a charming, kindly, and extremely gentle old canon. He had recently celebrated his golden jubilee in the priesthood—a truly noble record of devoted service in God's service. But he belonged to a different generation. Innovations of any sort were anathema to him. Provided the vestments were in a good state of preservation and the stock of candles properly maintained, all was well. The Children of Mary were kept going and encouragement given to the strictly religious guilds. But new movements, even those recommended by the Holy See, were not for his parish. They might be all well enough for some places, perhaps, but let the old, solidly established congregation rest in peace upon its well-earned laurels. That was the attitude.

It would have been quite easy for me to sit back and take life very easily. No existence could have been more pleasant. The housekeeper, although she tended to wear the parochial trousers, was kind and considerate to the curates. The table was always amply supplied with the choicest food, and the parishioners themselves were generous, as Catholics invariably are to their clergy. Many of them felt inclined to draw the line, however, at the housekeeper gallivanting off to another county in a hired car, paid for, they supposed, out of their offerings.

Again, the church itself was outstandingly beautiful and

the services were well performed. Yet I quickly perceived that beneath the deceptively smooth exterior things were actually very far indeed from satisfactory.

Within a mile there was, for example, a very large new housing development called the Raploch Estate, in which the overflow population from the old town had been re-housed. In it dwelled hundreds of nominal Catholics long lapsed from the Church; in fact, scarcely 5 per cent of the inhabitants attended to their religious duties, a most unusual state of affairs in the Catholic Church.

This housing estate was notorious for many miles around by reason of its dirty condition and high crime-rate. I made it a special point to spend not less than five hours each day visiting the area, and I endeavoured to cover the entire district at least twice a year. I trudged from street to street and from house to house. I truly loved that district and all its people, but oh, the degradation! I got a thousand special pamphlets printed and distributed them from door to door, in which I urged the people to a higher way of life, forcibly reminding them of their obligation to observe the Sabbath by resting from physical labour and attending to their religious duties. The Press referred to this operation as a "spiritual bombing campaign", and I am glad to add that results ensued almost at once, and a gradual improvement all round became evident.

The problem, however, was a complex one. The people were socially retarded; many of their homes were in a revolting state of filth. Walking round the area, I saw young children running about the streets in their bare feet, grimy from tip to toe and often with open sores on their heads. This infuriated me. Every summer a number of children were drowned in the nearby river, simply because parents were so disgustingly negligent that a child could wander away from its so-called home without its ever being noticed. I had to turn myself into a regular children's "nursemaid". Often on my rounds I had to rush into the roadway to pull some poor little child out of the danger of passing traffic. I would ask them where they lived, take them back to their neglectful parents, and issue a stern warning that in the event of a recurrence it would become a matter of calling in the National Society for the Prevention of Cruelty to Children. Where, however, it did not appear that the parents were to blame, I would enlist help to care for these young waifs.

Seldom did a day pass by without my being called to a hospital or a home for the purpose of consoling or strengthening those in trouble. One of the most touching experiences I remember was that of attempting to lead a distracted young mother away from the remains of her little boy, aged five, who had been drowned in the river. The episode pointed a lesson which constantly forces itself upon the attention of a pastor of souls: namely, that youth no less than age may at any moment be claimed by the grim reaper. Indeed, I received a bitter reminder of that truism when one of the most active and valuable of my youth leaders, the President of the Young Christian Workers, went out one Saturday afternoon to play another club at football and, on his return home, collapsed and died.

Another of my very sad experiences came when I was summoned to a house where a young mother had taken her life by swallowing poison. There were six very young and beautiful children left behind with a grief-stricken father; another had been on the way. I am not ashamed to say that the sight of them sitting forsaken and forlorn brought a flood of tears to my eyes. The body was removed; kindly neighbours went in to clean the rooms and, for a week or so, to feed the six little orphans. But this could not go on for ever. Even the most charitable neighbours tire in time, and the youngest child, aged eighteen months, required considerable attention.

The father was a helpless sort of fellow, as demonstrated by the fact that he had cheerfully built up a large family without taking into account his wife's failing health and her despair at the approaching arrival of a seventh mouth to feed. The more educated members of the Roman Church, of course, use birth-control techniques in spite of the authorities' stern law against such practices. But in large working-class dis-stricts the uninstructed, and often over-sexed partner exercises no restraint, either with or without modern facilities. There are, I realize, strong arguments to be advanced against contraceptives, but I maintain they also have a powerful case in their favour.

Anyway, something had to be done about those children, and as I was unable to find any family able to take them in, I packed them all into a large hired car and drove them seven miles to an orphanage. It was a bitterly cold January day, with the snow lying deep upon the ground. Several hundred yards before reaching the main gates of the institution, the car stuck in a drift, and beyond the gates there was still a long drive to be negotiated. The car proving inextricable, there was no alternative but to carry the children two at a time, and with the help of the chauffeur this was finally accomplished, and we landed the poor little orphans in the tender, welcoming arms of the Sisters of Mercy. Nor was this the sole occasion on which I had to bring derelict children to the doors of the orphanage. In fact, a time came when at last the good Sisters were driven to the point of remonstrating with me and begging me to put a curb upon my ardour as a collector of waifs and strays!

The Raploch Estate's population included a large number of young boys who had no club of any sort or description. With the help of the Education Committee I formed both a Senior and a Junior Club. Apart from the weekly activities, I took a hundred of the boys for a week's camping holiday by the sea each summer, and it was there, with the assistance of the leaders whom I myself trained, that we really had an opportunity to mould the boys' characters and come to know them as they really were rather than as they appeared to be at the weekly meetings. The boys would be housed in a large hall, and their food would be cooked by ladies of the parish who gave up their own holidays to assist without thought of remuneration.

But whatever work I undertook for unattached or non-religious youth, I did not neglect my regular duties. I steadily performed them to the utmost of my ability and went much farther than most of my colleagues. With no wish to boast, I feel bound to put on record that I got as much work done in a year as some clergy did in ten. Had I been content to sit in my armchair at the Clergy House, reading or dozing my time away, I might have escaped all trouble. Anxiety for the spiritual and moral welfare of the lost legions was destined to be my downfall. My unforgivable offence was that I refused to associate myself with the clerical trade-union attitude of "Do what you're told and no more!"

The position among the school-children was especially deplorable. Just before the War, a very large and beautiful school building had been erected for seven hundred Catholic children, and it had cost a small fortune. At the outbreak of hostilities, however, the Polish and other foreign armies had taken it over. The state in which they had left the magnificent structure defied all description. Upon taking up my duties I was horrified to find it still standing empty with most of its windows smashed and the walls hideously disfigured by the troops who had occupied it for three years. And added to this was the fact that thieves had broken into the premises and helped themselves wholesale to fittings and materials. Committees had been sitting on the problem for two years, but nothing had been done, and every day more panes of glass were being broken by vandals.

The pupils who should have been occupying this building were crowded meanwhile into an old structure only half the required size, a place I could only describe as a hovel. There they were, without room to move, and yet within a short distance stood the potential scholastic palace, all but a wreck. It made my blood boil to see this fantastic situation. While those supposed to be wiser and more experienced than I was were content to discuss the matter in Council, I thought up a plan to expedite the remedy. I rang up the biggest and most influential newspaper and found them interested. A reporter and a photographer duly arrived on the scene, and next day the middle page of the paper was filled with pictures of the two buildings side by side—the derelict palatial school contrasted with the tumbledown old premises crammed to the doors with children scarcely able to breathe! The Education Authorities gnashed their teeth with rage, but none the less, the building was renovated very soon afterwards.

Needless to say, I received no thanks, none even from the Ecclesiastical Authorities, whose urgent problem it really was. But then I neither expected thanks nor wanted any. It was ample reward to me that the children would soon have a decent school. Professional jealousy is a terrible thing among clergy and schoolmasters. Humanly speaking, it pays you to do nothing; it certainly keeps you out of trouble. Some people, however, cannot fit into this philosophy, and so their lives are a constant succession of ups and downs. They are for ever in and out of hot water. Their superiors suspect them of trying to usurp their places, while their colleagues suspect them of attempting to outshine them. Mediocrity is a comfortable couch, and the majority of men lie down and take their ease upon it. So far as I was concerned, however, I have always been in trouble with authorities, and probably always will be, in spite of a sincere desire to please.

Probably the most interesting venture upon which I embarked was the "Open Door" movement. Like so many towns of Scotland in those days, Stirling was very puritanical, in the sense that on Sundays all cinemas and other places of amusement were closed. Consequently, on Sunday evenings hundreds of young people drifted up and down the main streets with nothing particular to do, and thus exposing themselves to the many temptations which idleness and aimlessness inevitably present to the adolescent. The police were always out in strong force on Sunday evenings, but they could not be everywhere at once. Forbidden to dance or watch an innocuous movie, the young folk freely took advantage of the facilities offered by dark alleyways for fornication.

Although most of the religious denominations raised objections to opening cinemas or holding concerts on Sundays, they made no attempt to provide an adequate alternative for these young people, the majority of whom belonged to no particular creed, and as a consequence were recognized by nobody as a responsibility. Feeling very strongly that something must at least be attempted on their behalf, I rented a large room and formed a Sunday Youth Club with an initial membership of fifty. Within a fortnight it was crowded to the door.

Before long such a large number of youngsters were having to be turned away that I applied for the use of the lesser Town Hall. The Town Council eventually granted this, but with a good many strings attached, since the authorities showed themselves extremely strict as to the types of entertainment to be presented, objecting even to ordinary songs and sketches. I knew very well, of course, that it was no earthly use expecting the adolescents to patronize gatherings where the proceedings would be limited to singing hymns, as the City Fathers seemed to expect of them. They would have been in church instead of roaming the streets! It required great diplomacy and patience to weather the early storms. Eventually, however, prejudice was overcome and the Councillors won over to my point of view. From then on we staged talent competitions, quizzes, and all sorts of other events likely to appeal to the young people. Within a year they were producing their own concerts and other functions, and so popular had the meetings become that the membership shot up to three hundred, and I was forced to hire the large Town Hall. In the end the membership stood at more than eight hundred.

I felt more than rewarded when the Chief Constable publicly acknowledged that in consequence of my efforts he was now able to withdraw most of his men from the Sunday evening patrol. The streets were all but deserted. Nor were the activities of our Sunday Youth Club confined to the Sabbath, for during the week we held special meetings for discussion and general recreation.

It is difficult to believe that work such as that just described could possibly meet with opposition from people of goodwill. Nevertheless, the primary obstacle was not the difficulty of training these young people so lacking in background, or that of finding the necessary finance, but rather the attitude of those authorities who seemed to begrudge the success of our venture. Jealousy plays an ugly part in community life, and even among brother priests the green eye of envy destroys good work. All went well until a certain group of narrow-minded bigots complained to the Archbishop that Catholic and Protestant youth were serving together on the committee of our "Open Door" Movement, with the result that non-sectarianism was being encouraged at the expense of the Church.

Actually, the reputation of the Catholic Church in this formerly bigoted city stood higher than it had ever been previously. Hundreds of people who had always thought of Catholic priests and laymen as semi-demons with figurative horns and cloven hoofs discovered that they were in reality just very human neighbours willing to do something for the common good. But the ecclesiastical hierarchy "cared for none of these things". They resented one of their clergy working to help "outsiders", and the public authorities, having little or no sympathy with the type of youth whom we were striving to salvage, regarded the work as an embarrassment if not an actual nuisance.

Since those days the Authorities have come to realize that unless one sincerely and efficiently tackles this problem, the country is liable to inherit a legacy of juvenile delinquency. For with a more progressive and understanding attitude towards the unattached youth of all classes and creeds in the initial stages, society can be relieved of many subsequent and well-nigh insoluble problems.

But no such understanding attitude was to come about in the Stirling autocracy—far from it. It was evident that as time went on an increasing number of complaints regarding my activities were forwarded to Bishop's House; and it is a well-known fact that if sufficient mud is thrown at the same object over a long enough period of time, some of it is bound to stick. It was impossible for me not to know that this was going on. All I could do was to obey the voice within me which urged me on, to the best of my powers and in the way which seemed to me the only right way, towards a fuller realization of "Love your neighbour as yourself".

Looking back upon my priestly labours, as I have so often done in later years, I can recall few incidents of which I feel cause to be ashamed, or concerning which I can entertain any deep regret. One there was, however, which does stand out remorsefully in my memory. There was a notorious character in the parish whose favourite hobby was to wield the poison-pen. Her idiosyncrasy took the form of writing long and abusive letters to our housekeeper, of whom she was insanely jealous, or to the Canon, whom she accused of having persecuted her pet curates in the past. How the poor Canon could ever have been guilty of persecuting anybody I could not even begin to guess. It was fantastic, for the old dear was the very soul of charity—*too* kind, in fact. And I, who seemed always to have had my full share of hard masters, knew how to appreciate a good superior when I was fortunate enough to get one.

One day I myself received one of the venom-laden letters, a long one to the effect that the Canon was responsible for all the ills of the parish. I saw red; my loyalty was at stake. Off I tore to interview the wretched, ill-balanced woman. I fairly let verbal hell loose, tearing her asunder with my eloquence, and bludgeoning her with blow after blow of angry denunciation. Then I stalked out, leaving her to the recriminations of her conscience. . . . I had, of course, acted quite wrongly. What the poor soul needed was coaxing, soothing, and reassuring. The line I had taken, far from doing any good, had wrought only irreparable harm. The letters stopped, it is true. But they had been the unfortunate woman's safety-valve, and when they stopped her condition went from bad to worse.

The final stages of my sacerdotal career were heralded by the appearance at the Clergy House of an amazing character, Father Dordon Barbon. He had the reputation of being a sort of Roman Messiah, one at whose advent anywhere all troubles ceased forthwith. Miracles could be expected to solve, in a matter of days, difficulties which years of hard labour had failed to surmount. Physically he was a most substantial person—all thirty stone of him. Bluff, arrogant, officious, but fairly oozing with charm when he wanted something, he barged into the parish with all the delicacy of an outsize elephant.

At breakfast each morning the Canon was tackled as to what he intended doing about his parish. For a while the old warrior fought back, but the time came when he succumbed to the incessant badgering, and from then on Father Dordon ruled as regent in his stead. And this was precisely what the Archbishop had intended should happen.

For a time the obese regent was sweeter than honey in his bearing towards me, but gradually he discovered that my territories were not quite so easily to be annexed as Poland had been. Then trouble really began. Cold winds started to blow from the North-East, the location of Bishop's House. They reached their full force one morning when, on entering the Clergy House after celebrating Mass, I saw on the table a registered letter addressed to me in the Archbishop's scrawly hand. And evidently Father Dordon must have possessed pre-knowledge of its contents, for before I had even begun to open the envelope he fixed me with a malevolent eye and volunteered the opinion, in his usual harsh voice, that somebody "appeared to be in trouble".

Filled with a nameless foreboding, I left the table, carried the letter up to my room, and opened it. A blow between the eyes with a sledge-hammer could not have stunned me more effectively than what I read in the very first line of the letter:

"*You are hereby suspended from all duties as from this moment.*"

6

Temptations of the Flesh

"O though who did'st with pitfall and with gin
Beset the path I was to wander in!"
Rubáiyát of Omar Khayyám, EDWARD FITZGERALD

"Lust is preferred by foolish men only because of the immediateness of delight. . . . They heed not the suffering and the wretchedness that follow in its train, and therefore incline in accord with their natural impulses to the attainment of present pleasure."
The Choice of Pearls, IBN GABIROL. (7)

WHEN the initial numbness produced by this paralysing blow of my suspension began to pass off, my reaction to it took the form of blazing resentment. The Archbishop's apparently utter disregard of the constructive work that I had so painstakingly built up I could only see as a blatant injustice. To think that my zealous, sincere, and self-obliterating efforts to aid hundreds of my fellow creatures had brought not reward, not even recognition, but *disgrace*! I reminded myself how I had spent every penny of my slender material means on the furtherance of faith and religious work; how month after month I had worn myself out tramping the streets of slum districts and ministering to the lapsed, when I could so easily have had a perpetual sinecure and remained in favour; how I had extended my enthusiasm to embrace the ranks of the shepherdless, and that without attempting to convert them!

This last, I realized, had been my crime, and no crime could have earned a more drastic punishment. Untainted as I had succeeded in keeping myself, despite many a temptation, my life was smudged now with a stain which could never be completely erased. The Archbishop had destroyed me utterly with one fell blow!

Jesus could suffer the disgrace of a felon's death upon the Cross, I reflected bitterly, but I was not Jesus. Presumably the Archbishops were more advanced in their conception of justice than Christ's executioners had been. For my Christian superior, therefore, there was less excuse than there had been for the bigoted zealots of two thousand years ago.

Oh, yes, I was indeed feeling very, very sorry for myself!

The thought of the life so many other priests were leading—and getting away with—added fuel to my burning resentment. The vast majority, I well knew, led perfectly decent lives, but I was aware of several in that very diocese who were getting drunk weekly and living in flagrant immorality, yet nobody even thought of suspending them. I knew of one church administrator who was carried up to bed twice a week regularly by his long-suffering curates, soaked in whisky and swearing like a bargee. I was personally acquainted with one young priest who spent his free afternoons "necking" in the park with a good-looking young woman. Apparently the latter's mother did not object very strongly, and although numerous parishioners saw the amorous cleric's philandering in progress, none of them troubled to report it.

Then there was the case of a parish priest of whose immoral carryings-on I had positive knowledge. One day the housekeeper of the Church House where this priest resided came to one of the curates in a state of great agitation. A "loud creature of a woman, dressed up to the eyes in furs", she confided, had called at the door and demanded to see her "Tootles". The naughty father of the parish flock, it seemed, was himself something of a sheep, but a black one. He had stayed with the present visitor the previous Monday night, but had omitted to leave an honorarium, and she felt entitled to some material token of his gratitude for services rendered. Unless something was promptly arranged, the lady had added, she would certainly feel compelled to write to the Archbishop.

The housekeeper, a loyal soul if ever there was one, had with her own savings bought off this troublesome assuager of God's anointed. When I heard of this shameful episode I had wondered very much what would have happened to "Tootles" had His Grace heard of the painful tidings. And now, in my mood of bitterness, I told myself that the Archbishop could not have done much more to the errant pastor for his adultery—the woman was separated from her husband—than he had done to me for merely not minding my own business.

Even the diatribes against England publicly voiced by certain Irish fellow-priests had gone unreprimanded. Unlike their predecessors of the last generation, who had been most acceptable members of any community, scholarly, charitable, and broad-minded, these priests were very politically inclined. They used every opportunity in club or society to advance their nationalistic cause and sling abuse at the country which afforded them its hospitality and protection. The venom of their attitude, I had often thought, went ill with their profession of charity. Yet I had never heard of their rantings becoming the subject of even the mildest archiepiscopal rebuke.

Contrasting the conduct of all these notorious backsliders with what I will always regard as a purely technical malfeasance on my own part—and that only a malfeasance because of the Church authorities' narrow outlook—I flung myself down on my bed and gave way to unrestrained grief. Had God vanished from the universe, I demanded? How would He permit an Archbishop to commit so fiendish an act? I remained in my room without taking breakfast. Eventually the Canon entered in a state of evident distress to perform the unwelcome office of confirming the Archbishop's instructions. He did all in his power to comfort me, and after an hour or so's conversation he suggested that I should go on a short vacation until the Archbishop's wrath had abated. He assured me that the tyrannical prelate, once he had taken time to reflect upon the situation, would relent. It was obvious, he said, that His Grace had acted in a moment of fury, egged on by his vicious sycophants. He was a creature of impulse, prone to take action without due consideration.

Accepting this advice, and having drawn my month's salary, I set out for London. By this time I had recovered from my initial shock, and to tell the truth I even felt somewhat relieved by my departure. At least, I told myself, I would not be under the gloating eye of Father Dordon. Furthermore, had I remained in the parish while under suspension, inquisitive busybodies would have been pestering me with all sorts of questions. The situation, in fact, would have proved impossible.

As the train sped on its way, I even began in a vague sort of fashion to feel that this apparent knock-out blow might perhaps point the way towards an answer to my so oft-recurrent doubts. Frequently in history men had needed a crisis, or even a downright disaster, to lead them to their true destinies. It might well be so in my own case.

Although I no longer felt able to pray because my heart was too full of bitterness, I could at least comfort myself with the assurance that, no matter what might happen, my faith in God was not extinct. True, my accustomed facility in addressing myself to my Creator had temporarily deserted me. But my belief in Him was unimpaired. Though this was the one thing of which I could feel certain, it was a great deal in my state of mind at the time.

With Christianity, however, it was a different matter entirely. More strongly than ever I felt the conviction that Jesus had been not only a Jew by birth but a *practising* Jew, though one who did what thousands of other Jews have done since: namely, objected to certain interpretations of Jewish law and endeavoured to make Judaism more liberal. The first Christians had prayed in synagogues. Then came Paul, shrewdly appreciative of the fact that although the pagan world was ready for a more advanced form of faith, it was not ready for pure monotheism as expressed in Judaism, nor would be for many, many ages to come. And accordingly, he had taken the foundations laid by Jesus and developed them into a world religion for the Gentiles.

In short, Paul had invented what I called "Judaism for export". He had realized that the world would accept the conception of One God provided there was a flavour of Hellenism to render it more or less tangible. The Gentiles must have their images, their prayers to mediators, and their colourful ritual and liturgy—their sugar plums, in fact. It was a step in the right direction, but no more than a step, and even that had been followed by a retrogression. For the dogmas of the Church had in course of time been added, and an elaborated system of belief had evolved with the centuries. The teachings of Jesus the Jew and the dogmas of the all-powerful Church were worlds apart. Christianity, as thus evolved, and particularly the Roman brand, relied far too much on external props and consolations. Nor had it retained the attitude of universal love and sympathy so constantly stressed by Jesus. As I knew only too well from my own experience, religious people, even religious leaders, could be devilishly cruel.

Eventually, I was sure, the world would shed its artificially contrived religious media and go straight to God Himself. And I knew now with dazzling clarity that I was about to cut history short in my own lifetime—to return to Mount Zion, where I would once again hear the Word transmitted by the mouth of Moses: "I am the Lord thy God; thou shalt have no gods before me."

Arriving in London I lost no time in ringing up a cousin of mine with whom I had always been particularly friendly. From time to time Martin and I had met in Town and had gone to the theatre together. He had come South to establish a branch of the family business, and was making a success of it. He was a heathen if ever there was one, but he was the only relative who had refrained from abusing me for not only joining the Roman Church but also spending ten years of my life studying for its priesthood. I felt I could not wish for a more effective antidote to my present *malaise* than his company. I told him in brief outline what had happened, and he promptly insisted on my coming to stay with him.

It was a relief to pour out my woes into a sympathetic ear, and I let Martin have it in good measure. Had I done what some of my less-zealous brethren had done and allowed the masses of unattached youth to wander unhindered into hell, I declared, all would have been well. Had I even been carried upstairs stone-drunk or gone to bed with one of the Children of Mary, all would have been excused. I might possibly, I supposed, have been rebuked by the almighty prelate, but it was doubtful in the extreme whether I would have been suspended, as had happened the previous day. Were it only possible to escape from the same planet as was inhabited by priests, nuns, and all other nauseatingly pious creatures, I wound up, I would gladly do so, but as matters were I would have to do the next best thing.

Martin heard me out to the end of my tirade. Then he reminded me: "I told you years ago, you silly blighter, what would happen if you got caught up in that priest racket."

The apartment was comfortable, bright, and warm, and Martin, like the good fellow he was, gave up his own room to his distraught, dejected cousin in the dog-collar and himself took the smaller room. For an hour we sat chatting by the fire. I could sense that Martin had gauged my mood, and I freely unloaded all my troubles. What a change for one who had spent so many years listening to the troubles of others!

Martin was a gay, irreligious young man-about-town, well accustomed to tasting the pleasures of metropolitan life, both legitimate and otherwise. He listened patiently to my outpouring until at last, struggling against an impulse to cry like a baby, I came to an end. And then he proceeded to apply the remedy which seemed obvious to him, being the kind of young man he was.

"Now just you listen to me, old boy," he began. "I've no wish to discuss religion, and I'm damned sure you haven't either just now. If you want to get over this shock and stay sane, there's just one way to do it. You've got to forget everything that's past until you can make up your mind what you're going to do. And in the meantime my place is yours for as long as you need it. . . . But tonight you and I are going out. And don't for one moment imagine I'm going to lug you round in that devil-dodger's outfit of yours, either. You need a complete break, so go and get into one of my suits and make yourself respectable. Then we'll make a night of it."

Had such a suggestion been put to me a month or so previously, and in such robust language, I am sure I would have refused with some indignation. But now every fraction of my erstwhile respect for my superiors and pride in my clerical status had gone with the wind. After a few drinks—and this, too, was something quite abnormal for me—I went and changed into my cousin's more worldly garments, a transformation which undeniably made me feel a great deal better.

We set out for the West End, and I assumed that Martin was going to prescribe the distraction of a theatre. But that, it seemed, was not to be the programme. Martin announced, in fact, that the first item of business was to get a few more drinks under our belts. He was evidently bent on making my temporary lapse from holiness a thorough one, and I got the impression that in spite of his anger at the treatment meted out to me, he was rather enjoying his rôle in the unexpected drama. And all the more so, I guessed, because, although he had not joined in my other relatives' condemnation of my going over to Rome, he had none the less heartily disapproved of it.

For a start we called in on Martin's particular set, a group of young people who came together regularly at one another's houses or flats for a night's enjoyment. Since they had no idea of my real identity or calling, my mixing in presented no problem.

"This will give you a chance to see the world through the other end of the telescope," Martin impressed upon me. "Just bear in mind that tonight you're one of them, not preaching to them."

I had no desire whatsoever to preach to them. As I squatted in a corner, surrounded by young people who were drinking, smoking, chatting, singing, exchanging lighthearted banter, and in some cases openly "necking", I contrasted the kindly, charitable outlook on life of these youthful pagans with the crabbed "holier than thou" attitude of the pious people with whom I had been associating myself. It all seemed so incongruous, yet so easily understandable that this way of life should detest the other.

Martin's young associates knew nothing of me, but judging from their warm attitude, it might well have been that they sensed my need for comforting. They were the very essence of friendliness and bent over backwards to make me feel at home. I had in my time given consolation to 'teen-agers by the hundred, many of them quite without any particle of religion in their make-up. Now it was they who, all unwittingly were pouring balm upon the professional comforter's wounded heart and mind. I reflected that if only religious people were more pleasant and more human, there would be far more of them in the world. Why was it that the devotees of religion were so frequently harsh, unattractive, and even cruel? Perhaps that had been the trouble with Jesus, who was up against the ultra-religious sect of His day.

How glad I was to be where I know found myself, though! The grim figure of the mitred despot was beginning to fade into the hazy background, a figure almost beyond imagination in this carefree, bohemian atmosphere. I drank down whatever was put into my hand and felt the strain and desperation of the last two days lifting. This was not such a bad life, after all! Following years of study and association with "squares", not to say straitlaced spiritual snobs, with their perpetual output of bitter zeal, I was glad to sit in a crowd of young people possibly not overburdened with virtue, but at least free from the religious vice of what is unjustly termed Phariseeism.

What surprised and delighted me most of all in these adolescents was their basic decency. They drank in moderation, they swore, they petted, they blasphemed, but they were none the less charitable and clean. I preferred every one of their weaknesses to the ruthless, merciless, narrow-minded absolutism of those who considered themselves the Lord's anointed, and whose very guts I had come to hate!

Poor God, I thought. He has such unattractive salesmen in His holy business. No wonder these young spirits would not buy the Ten Commandments or any other part of Christianity in general. Dog-collars, black hats, umbrellas, and back-biting held no glamour for them. They intended to *live*. Perhaps a dozen live wires such as Dick Sheppard might have saved this generation for Church or Synagogue, but clerical professionalism spelled bunkum for them. Almost my entire generation of those born during the years immediately preceding the Second World War were lost to organized religion. Not only did they not attend church, chapel, or synagogue, but they showed no sign of being even vaguely aware that such institutions existed. Things of that sort belonged to the era of tramcars, hansom cabs, and the Crystal Palace. These thousands of latter-day Elizabethans simply did not include religion in their world. They had their own code of conduct. Certain things were "not done"—usually the kind of things that hurt other people's susceptibilities. The religious set, by contrast, would not hesitate to trample ruthlessly on the feelings of a neighbour who failed to observe all the requirements of their sanctimonious "respectability". As they marched sedately churchwards, bowler hatted, bespatted, umbrella in hand, and with measured tread, bent on displaying the fulfilment of their religious duties, they saw the masses—especially the masses of youth—as a collection of jungle-dwellers such as only fools or sinners would bother even to consider.

Such were the very naughty, worldly thoughts that passed through my mind. "If only that old so-and-so could see me now," I chuckled to myself, "dressed in the latest style of Savile Row and sitting sandwiched among a group of lovely girls in velvet pants!" What more could he have done to me,

I wondered. I would have hardly objected to a suspension in payment for my present enjoyment. And since I already was suspended, why not justify in good measure the punitive action taken by my Father-in-God?

So I sat, thinking to myself and chatting animatedly, until at last I caught a wink from Martin indicating that the time had come for us to move on. In this congenial company the hours had slipped by faster than I had realized. As the door closed behind us I thanked Martin for the experience.

"Just the same," was that young man-of-the-world's rather unexpected reply, "you might have cashed in on it a bit more than you did!"

Failing in my naïveté to catch his point, I protested that I had thoroughly enjoyed myself.

"But not thoroughly enough for my liking," my cousin grunted. "That peach of a blonde sitting next to you by the piano was all set for fun and games. What made you get cold feet?"

"Give a fellow a chance," I pleaded, not quite certain whether to feel shocked or flattered. "I mean to say, not too much all at once, you know!"

"Now listen to me," said Martin, adopting the tone of a Dutch uncle. "If you don't fall before next week-end there's going to be hell to pay. You needn't imagine I'm going to let you go back to sit behind bars again in that Holy Joe monkey-house of yours up in Stirling. You've been suppressed more than enough for a lifetime. So chuck it now and start living! All these years you've been sweating your guts out for a bunch of ungrateful boors. If you do go back, remember, then I'm with the rest of the family and we are through."

I was upset by this stern and uncompromising attitude on Martin's part. After all, we were more like brothers than cousins, and he represented the sole remaining link with my family. If that link were to be severed, as Martin was warning me that it well might be, I would feel isolated in all conscience. I kept silent, however, and presently Martin spoke again.

"Sorry if I've said anything to hurt you, old boy," he said gruffly, "but when I saw you break down like that up in the apartment I just saw red! I know you've never done a rotten thing in your life. You're the last person in the world who should be treated so damnably!"

"That's all right, Martin," I answered, more than a little touched by his solicitude on my behalf. "I just need time to think and get adjusted, that's all."

"O.K., let's forget it," said Martin. And with that he thrust his arm through mine and steered me in the direction of Soho. Nor did he allow me to remain long in doubt as to what his ideas were for my further education in the ways of the world. I couldn't help guessing from the words he let drop as we walked along, guarded though they were, just what form his intentions took. He doubtless wished to precipitate a clean break—if "clean" is the right adjective!—with my other-worldly past. Such an experience as he contemplated for me, he presumably reasoned, might shake me out of my groove and force a decision. And once free of the priesthood, he hinted, I could then either go into the business or perhaps start a school, as another member of the family had done successfully. On the other hand, if he allowed me to go back to the priesthood, anything might happen. As he said, in another outburst of anger, the religious authorities had unjustly disgraced me, and he did not wish them to have a second chance of breaking me beyond repair. Already they had all but crushed the life out of me, "the sanctimonious, totalitarian, Gadarene swine!" Evidently in Martin's peculiar recollection those swine were the lowest of all the porcine species.

Eventually Martin came right to the point, suggesting in plain terms that I should get the horrible business out of my system by having sexual relations with a member of the opposite sex. It wasn't a thing he normally believed in, he went on to explain; in fact, he himself had had only one such experience. But in my case, he felt, it would be "just what the doctor ordered", a shock-treatment calculated to bring me down to earth.

I protested that promiscuity of that nature simply held no appeal for me, purely as a matter of fastidiousness and quite apart from the fact that willy-nilly I was still a priest. Martin, however, made short shrift of my objections.

"You're in bad shape," he insisted, "and extreme cases call for extreme remedies. You've simply got to get that pent-up fury of yours worked off. And besides, you haven't had all that much fun and games out of holiness, have you? Come on, be human for once!"

So on we walked into Wardour Street, one of the better known sin-streets of London, with Martin casting a connoisseur's eye over the various traders in sex whom we passed on our way. I noticed that the majority of these women's clients seemed to be men over thirty years of age; scarcely once did I spot any in their 'teens or early twenties. For the most part they created the impression of married men who had either quarrelled with their wives and wanted to get their own back, as they saw it, or who merely sought a "change of bowling". In a sort of a way I found myself in sympathy with them, having married an institution which had broken my heart! Furthermore, to say that I felt no temptation at all, now that we were in the heart of the market in human flesh, would not be strictly true; for when all was said and done I was a man, with a man's natural appetites, and if I could have smothered my qualms I might have been willing to go the whole hog. But smother them I could not, and I had not the remotest intention of falling in with Martin's well-meant plans for my salvation.

We came to a point where a strikingly pretty girl stood in a shop entrance. She had a wonderful figure, and the "come hither" smile she gave us looked frank and friendly rather than purely professional. Martin, cool as a cucumber, came to a halt and opened the negotiations without further ado.

"Hullo, sweetheart," he said, "how about giving my pal here a good time? I'll make it worth your while."

"You mean just a short time?" the damsel queried. "That'd be a couple of pounds."

But Martin waved away any such petty proposition.

"No, no, that's no use," he declared. "I want him to stay with you all night."

"In that case it'll set you back five guineas," the trader announced in a business-like manner. "That O.K.?"

"It's a deal," said Martin. And he added, grabbing hold of my arm, "Go to it, old boy; it's all yours!"

While this cold-blooded bargaining was in progress I had grown more and more uncomfortable, and by this time I was bathed in perspiration.

"No, really, thanks," I stammered out in my agony of embarrassment. "To tell the truth, I'm not feeling too good. Let's just go for a drink, shall we?"

"Well, make up your mind, ducks," prompted the lady. "Plenty more nice boys around, you know!"

Martin must have realized that he had lost the first round, for without further ado he bade the beauty a curt farewell and piloted me away, looking anything but pleased.

"You're a bloody fool if ever there was one!" he muttered in a tone of exasperation. "You'll never feel right again, I keep telling you, until you've gone off the deep end completely. Get the whole blasted affair out of your system, and then you can settle down. But not in the damned priesthood; you're through with that racket for good and all, do you hear? Be a man and live a normal life. Everyone has to kick over the traces once in a while. You've been a lifeless figure in a stained-glass window all your life, and it's time you knew it!"

"But listen a moment, Martin," I expostulated. "I'm not judging you or anyone else. I realize perfectly well, especially just now, that some of the nicest people in the world are those who don't give a tinker's damn for religion or conventional morality. But it's just that I'm not made that way, I suppose. It's something I can't bring myself to do, and that's all there is to it."

"You represent a pretty small minority, old boy," Martin told me. "We've left all that sort of rubbish behind long ago, you know."

"I don't believe that," I stubbornly maintained. "I'm sure most people still think that pre-marital intercourse is wrong, even if they have an occasional lapse."

"Well, have it your own way," Martin laughed good-humouredly. "But how about your priests? Are *they* all that scrupulous?"

"I'm pretty certain the majority are," I replied, "though of course I know there are a few who do stray from the straight and narrow."

"What you say may be true enough here in England," said Martin, "but I happen to know it's another story on the Continent."

"I can't argue with you on that point," I answered, "but I'm convinced that taking it by and large the Catholic priests live pretty decent lives."

"And hellish good reason *you* of all people have to defend the b——rs!" my cousin exploded. And when I protested that fair was fair even where my persecutors were concerned, he only vouchsafed an indignant snort. "Anyway, we need a drink after that fiasco," he grumbled, "so let's find some place where there's a little life."

We entered the saloon bar of a large tavern, and it speedily became manifest that Martin, having unwillingly saved five pounds on account of his relative's infuriating inhibitions, was determined to lash out in another direction.

"Two double whiskys, two double gins, and a pack of Old Gold," he promptly ordered. He knew that I was a non-smoker, and that such an unaccustomed quantity of alcohol would be quite beyond my capacity, although he had met Catholic padres during the War and had good reason to remember their outstanding prowess with the bottle. But he had lost one skirmish and had no intention of losing another one.

This time I had no serious moral objections to offer. And besides, I reflected, Martin had suffered one disappointment already, and a further lack of co-operation might prove too much. With this crisis I stood badly in need of my own flesh and blood. My religious "family" had spat on me for no reason, and I was grateful to have this pagan relative who, whatever his weaknesses, had a warm spot in his heart for me and sincerely wanted to be of help. His remedies might not be of the highest order, but the motives which prompted them were of the purest.

Our liquor having been consumed, and half of the cigarettes having been smoked by me—more or less under compulsion, I may add—we set off for home, somewhat unsteady of gait but light of heart. Arrived at the flat, we were either too tired to undress or incapable of doing so, I cannot say which, and both tumbled on to Martin's bed, where we slept peacefully until noon the following day.

Martin was already in the bath when I awoke. He had promised to take me to his tailor to get measured for some suitable clothes, and that night we were to go to a dance, where he would introduce me to some attractive girls. I excused myself from the visit to the tailor, however, telling Martin that I would get a job and then pay cash for a ready-made suit. I was anxious not to sponge on my over-generous cousin. And there was another and more cogent reason besides. Although I dared not tell this to Martin, who might be disposed almost to murder me if I did, I was secretly considering a return to the parish for a final trial.

Since Martin had to look in at his factory that afternoon, I took the opportunity to be alone with my thoughts. For hour after hour I wrestled with my problem. In the company of my cousin I was truly happy for the first time in years. He was so kind, so infallibly considerate; for example, that very morning he had slipped a few pound notes into my wallet while I slept, so that I should not have to undergo the humiliation of asking for money! And conversely, my affection for Martin was matched by a burning hatred of my dog-collar, the Archbishop, and all things religious. Regarding the matter from a purely human point of view, therefore, I had every reason to stay where I was.

Yet there was one strong reason why I felt I had to do the seemingly impossible. My quarrel with authority was not, in itself, a sufficient excuse for clearing out. Other clergy, some of them in high positions, had feuded violently with His Grace and still remained. If, moreover, I was to leave the ranks of the priesthood, it must be from complete conviction, and I must have time to search thoroughly for an alternative. Some men might be capable of living without a faith, but I was not one of them. No, the selfish short cut was too easy. Had I taken it, I could never afterwards have felt satisfied or at peace with myself.

There was, of course, the plausible excuse of disbelief concerning certain dogmas of the Church—that very disbelief which had assailed me for so long. But even saints had been thus tormented. I had to be certain, beyond the faintest shadow of doubt, that I was right in giving up the way of life and the serious responsibilities in preparation for which I had spent so many years of earnest study.

By the time I was due to go out and meet Martin for the evening's entertainment, I had made up my mind that on the following Monday—it was now Saturday—I would put on those damned clericals again and return to my priestcraft.

7

Discipline before Judaism

"They also serve who only stand and wait."
On His Blindness, JOHN MILTON

". . . The three times of daily prayer . . . is for his soul what nourishment is for his body."
Kuzari, 3 (2–5), JUDAH HALEVY. (8)

I HAD arranged to meet Martin at the Corner House, and as I made my way there my heart was heavy within me—as heavy as lead at the prospect of Monday's return to Clergy House. Meanwhile, I kept thinking that I might as well get what fleeting happiness I could in Martin's uninhibited company.

We duly arrived at the dance, and for a while I sat quietly enjoying the sight of the carefree couples and wishing I had learned to dance myself. But once again my scheming cousin had other ideas for me. Without a word of warning he came up to me with a very attractive girl in tow and calmly announced that she would teach me the steps and pilot me round the floor. To say that I was scared stiff would be an understatement; but not wishing to offend either Martin or the girl, I fell in with the proposal with the best grace I could muster. Under my partner's skilful guidance I managed rather better than I had expected, but when the music stopped I breathed a sigh of relief.

A sterner test, however, was still to come. No sooner was the dance over than Martin, obviously pleased with the success of his stratagem, and all unsuspecting of the resolution I had taken, came hurrying over to me again.

"I say, old boy," he announced, "I'm most awfully sorry, but I've got to take my partner home. Would you mind seeing Julie to her house, and then we'll meet back at my place?"

What could the bashful sheep in wolf's clothing do but stammer out how delighted he would be to escort the charming girl to her door? And duly escort her there I did, finishing up with a friendly chat outside her home. When I arrived at the flat I found Martin had just got back himself. He was agog to hear all about my supposed adventures.

"I bet she warmed you up a bit, didn't she?" was his leading question. "Pretty hot number, eh?"

Rather than disappoint him, I indulged in the rarity of a little white lie.

"She's all that," I agreed. "One of the hottest I've struck."

"I hope you didn't just let her go in without even kissing her?" Martin persisted.

"I should say not!" I fibbed with what I hoped was a suitable show of indignation at such a suggestion. "What do you take me for? I stood kissing her for a good ten minutes!"

"Good boy, you're coming on," approved my relative.

We rose late next morning. Martin teased me about not being in church to take services, then went off into a most un-Sundayish string of maledictions on the Archbishop and his tyrannical gang. That afternoon we saw a movie, then in the evening we went to a jazz session at the home of one of Martin's numerous friends.

It was with a heavy heart that I sat down late that night to write a farewell note to the cousin who had been so much more than a source of consolation to me in my hour of need. Indeed, it is not too much to say that Martin had probably saved me from a complete nervous and physical collapse.

> "Please forgive me," I wrote, "but I must go back to my chosen state of life, to make quite certain of my final decision. The unjust and cruel action of the Archbishop cannot be an adequate reason for rejecting everything for which I prepared so long and at such great sacrifice.
>
> "My days here with you saved me from complete blackout. Never shall I be able to repay the debt of gratitude I owe you. We do not see eye to eye on some issues, but one thing I have surely learned, and that is that the

non-religious are often more Godlike than the pious. I would rather live with you and your friends (bless them!) than with most of the religious humbugs I have met so far.

"You will never know how near I was to staying with you in your world, and it is only against my entire human nature that I return to the priesthood. God bless you always!"

When I had finished packing I made myself a simple breakfast. And then I sat down to rest and reflect once more before going to the station. Yes, I concluded, I would go back, albeit in disgrace, and work out this crushing problem to its final solution. If my doubts passed away, well and good; should they fail to do so, then I would return to the lay life with a clear conscience and, I hoped, a clear plan for the future.

I arrived at the station, settled myself in an empty carriage, and lapsed again into meditation. It would be a great mistake, I told myself, to come back to the parish with my tail between my legs. My only guilt was that of being charitable to outsiders. Was not that precisely what the Founder of Christianity had always advocated—to care for the lost sheep which were not of His fold? I thought again of the various clergy who might so much more easily and justly have been subjected to my present outlawed condition. Yet I knew now that my resentment and blazing anger would pass with time. Martin had released within me the danger of explosion, and nobody else could have done it so effectively. I had been in no mood to listen to clerical platitudes or the aphorisms of Job's comforters, who would have impressed upon me how wicked it was to be on the wrong side of the fence. They would have stressed preference for a sin of the flesh to a sin of pride. Religious people were probably the only ones I would not have listened to during the crisis; they would have merely precipitated disaster. For had I encountered any such hypocrites, I would certainly have told them all to go to hell and take their piety with them.

Yes, the wordly sanity of my beloved cousin and the young people around him had been the only possible medicine. Had I not been as convinced of God's existence and reality as I was of my own, I would cheerfully have thrown all religion overboard and joined the kindly, decent pagans who had no time for all this cant.

With these and kindred thoughts in mind, I dozed off. In my uneasy slumber I retraced the succession of milestones in the long journey that had brought me to my present situation. Once more I was the small choirboy obsessed with the ambition to enter the ministry. Then I found myself robing for my ordination. Scenes of my parochial activities passed in endless succession through my dreams. Again I experienced the delight of my success in caring for drifting youth. Again I went through the shock and humiliation of reading the Archbishop's sentence of suspension. . . . At that I woke with a jerk. And as the train sped onwards, carrying me to my unwelcome interview with His Grace, the bitterness was already fading with the prospect of other horizons. Dark my mind still was, but a faint light was peeping through. I knew now that if I should be unable to reconcile myself with my present professed faith or state of life, a new world would be dawning for me—the world of the Old Testament.

When eventually I arrived back at Clergy House, I found a message awaiting me instructing me to appear before the Archbishop immediately. The meeting was brief and to the point. His Grace, having now calmed down somewhat and partially recovered from his outburst of Highland temper, solemnly recapitulated the acts of disobedience of which he considered the wayward curate had been guilty. For my part I maintained a discreetly tongue-tied attitude, merely awaiting removal of the ban. This presently followed, bestowed with an infuriating air of self-conscious magnanimity, and I was free to return to my labours in my former parish.

I could not have cared less. Instead of the relief, gratitude, and sense of restoration to favour with which a year or so earlier I would have welcomed the lifting of such an embargo, I felt absolutely nothing. In place of prostrating myself with murmurs of delight, I nodded in stony silence. The restoration of my status was quite meaningless. Had the Archbishop decided to suspend me indefinitely, I would have welcomed rather than resented it. As I walked out of his study, I knew that I was already a stranger to everything associated with my calling. Physically I was still in the Church and its priesthood; spiritually I was moving towards a new home.

Anger had given place to sheer indifference. I knew now that the crisis had been only the opening of the sluice-gates to let forth a mighty, dammed-up flood which would carry me out of my deep entrenchment. The doubts had been there ceaselessly all the while, though held in abeyance by strenuous activity. It had required only a forceful explosion to bring them to the surface, and unwittingly the Archbishop had supplied the required impetus to set this off.

Stepping forth into the bright, crisp morning, I heartily wished myself back in London. Why had I been so foolish as to return and place myself once again in this intolerable position? Tomorrow morning I would have to go to the altar and offer Mass. Only too well I knew that when I uttered the vital words "*Hoc est Corpus Meum*"—"This is My Body"—they would ring true neither in my ears nor in my heart.

And the reality was even more painful than I had imagined it. It was sheer hell to me every time I sat in Confession and listened to some poor soul relating sins which I realized could properly be confided only to God. Then, too, the statues of Mary and the innumerable saints who claim devotion from the simple Catholic worshippers were more and more a source of offence to me. They constituted barriers which stood between the soul and its Creator.

There was, in fact, a very, very deep conviction in my

heart that this return to the priestly status was to be of the briefest duration. My conscience was no longer clean. I felt myself in an utterly false position. I wondered miserably how long I could go on.

After a few weeks I was transferred to another field of work. The parishioners gave me a touching farewell—so obviously sincere, in fact, that insensibly the reproach under which I had so unjustly suffered was dissolved in their gratitude and affection. But the glow of warmth this kindled in me was just as quickly chilled. The new parish was in the drab, uninspiring industrial town of Kirkcaldy, in Fifeshire, Scotland, surrounded at all times by that odious smell of linseed oil. The church was small and dingy, there were no prospects of facilities for useful labour. Nevertheless, I made the best of things, working hard in visiting the sick and gathering together the local youth.

It was shortly after my move to this fresh parish that the Archbishop died. I went to his lying-in-state, and I have already said how profoundly impressed I was by the paradox of this lifeless, almost inglorious figure who so recently had with one word been able to change the whole current of his subjects' lives. All the glory of the episcopal state lay there in that humble coffin.

His Grace's successor would eventually be appointed, and the future was entirely unprejudiced. I could build up a new and stronger life in a new episcopal reign. But I knew that there was no possibility for this. Every day I found it increasingly more difficult to carry out my sacred duties. Mass was a positive nightmare. As the moment of Consecration drew near, my mind would fill with horror at the prospect of lifting on high the Sacred Host, my ears filled with the clanging of the sanctuary bell and the voices of the semi-prostrated worshippers as they uttered those awful words, "My Lord and my God." For a person who sincerely believed that the bread and wine had become the body and blood of Christ there was, of course, no absolute idolatry. But for those who addressed a piece of bread as "My Lord and my God" without any such belief it surely was blasphemy of the most appalling nature.

A further complication lay in the preparation and reception of converts. I had in my time received quite a large number of Protestants into the Catholic Church, and I think I may say without boasting that I was known as a sympathetic though thorough instructor. Actually, I had frequently refused, even against the wishes of my fellow clergy, to receive into the Church candidates concerning whose deep and sincere convictions I was dubious. This applied particularly to cases of mixed marriages, when a Protestant was required to sign papers solemnly promising that all children of the union, whether boys or girls, would be educated in the Roman faith. This stipulation has given rise to considerable bitterness on the part of non-Catholic authorities, who regard it as a form of coercion, and the Church of England has taken a very dim view of it. Moreover, in practice, it was liable to be something of a farce, as the non-Catholic, being in love with the Catholic party, would so often sign anything just to get the business over and done with.

As time went on, I refused to take converts, pleading overwork and other excuses. Whenever an inquirer for reception into the Church came to me, I would tell him or her to come back in six months' time. And in the meantime, being less busily occupied than before, I read widely and deeply, finding the works of such writers as Professor Klausner and others more and more enlightening. My conviction that Judaism, with its pure, unsullied monotheism, was to be my destined goal grew ever firmer and more pressing. Night after night I lay awake wrestling with the problem that had now become urgent and immediate. Sleep would not come. An inner voice gave me no respite. "Get thee out, get thee out!" it kept urging. It was the voice of conscience; no human voice could have been clearer or more insistent.

Several times I started to pack my belongings, but always

in the morning I unpacked again. Where, after all, could I go in such a hurry? I was well aware that the Jewish authorities would take no action until some considerable time after I had made the break. I wanted desperately to cross my Rubicon and make myself a participant in the Jewish way of life, but as yet there was no bridge. I felt like a trapped animal.

Each day I hated my present position more. I despised myself for my cowardice and vacillation; but did God, I asked myself, expect me simply to walk out and starve? It was not so easy for an ex-priest to earn his living in another sphere. There was nothing I loved more than teaching, and I thought I might possess a flair for it, but who would accept me in that capacity? I could, of course, become a manual labourer and earn a good wage, but I was a student and not physically strong. Nor could I turn to my family for help, well-to-do though they were. They had already been deeply offended by my joining the Catholic Church; a transition to Judaism would certainly be considered the last straw.

It was all very difficult, but my priesthood was more than difficult—it had become impossible. I knew that I could never bring myself to stand before the altar again. Neither could I ever again climb into the pulpit to preach of mysteries which no longer meant anything to me. How was I to administer to the faithful what they believed to be the body and blood of Jesus, but which I now saw purely as bread and wine? And would it not be the very depth of hypocrisy to sit in the Confessional listening to those secrets which I was now so sure should be for God's ear alone?

There came a night when I knew I could not, dare not, celebrate another single Mass. Thus, I had been acting in error for a long time, but always there had been that vague, lingering remnant of doubt. Now there was no longer any doubt, not the minutest shred. I was already a Jew at heart; I believed in the Law of Moses. I utterly rejected all foundations of Catholicism—the Virgin Birth, the Trinity, the

Sacraments, and all the other paraphernalia of accumulated dogma.

Century after century, I argued the Church had kept on defining new doctrines. There had been the Infallibility of the Pope; the Assumption of the Virgin into Heaven; the Immaculate Conception. According to the Church, these dogmas had really been there all the time. But it was amazing how she had to stand on her head to prove it! How many more dogmas, I wondered, would the faithful be called upon to swallow before the final deposit of Faith was complete?

Well, that was all water under the bridge now, for the end of the struggle—or at all events of the first phase of it—had come. I recognized now what I had to do, though I still did not know how I was to do it. But surely the Lord who had called me would not leave me stranded at the parting of the ways? Surely He would indicate the road my feet must follow?

So I squared my spiritual shoulders, as it were, and assured myself that God would *not* desert me. "Bale out and trust in Him!" must be my slogan. Early next morning, therefore, I wrote a brief note in which I said nothing of my plans to embrace Judaism, since I was anxious to give no one a handle for anti-Semitism. I merely pleaded reasons of health to account for my departure. Then I packed my suitcase yet again, said my prayers, and set forth in search of a bridge to carry me over the flood. Without position, friends, promises, or any other form of security, I was leaving behind in that moment what I had spent years to gain. It was well that I could not see all the difficulties that awaited me ahead, for at the prospect of them I believe human courage would have failed the stoutest heart.

Even at this early stage I was faced with a serious problem, that of finance. In the past I had been able to command some material resources, but my education for the priesthood had swallowed up hundreds of pounds. Although when I entered the Bede Pontifical College I still had almost a thousand pounds to my credit, after paying all my fees and costs of maintenance after my ordination, not to mention assisting various projects, I had practically nothing left. And a devoted priest does not save much money. He has endless calls upon his purse, and he meets them. Moreover, having no wife and family to support relieves him of any urgent need to save. So he usually spends or gives away everything he gets. Although it was my intention to enter the Jewish communion, I knew beyond all question that it would be most unwise, as well as useless, to appeal to the Jewish authorities for help at this stage. Later on they might be willing to assist, but it was up to me now to make my own way out of "Egypt" and to cross the figurative Red Sea. At the other side some friendly hand might be stretched out to pull me ashore, but I would be expected to prove myself first. No help would be forthcoming until the authorities could be sure of my motives and complete conviction.

My faith in Providence had not been misplaced: it did provide a bridge. For fortunately my background, and especially my family background, stood me in good stead. Almost sooner than I could have dared to expect, I secured a post in the Junior House of Clayesmore, the Public School in Dorset. Better still, although the school's official faith was Anglicanism and I made it clear that I was not a member of the Church, I was entrusted with the duties and responsibilities of becoming one of the Housemasters there.

The staff represented a truly colourful array of personalities. As is the case with the majority of boarding schools, they were mostly of amateur status, though none the less highly qualified. Indeed, our public schools in England are almost devoid of the training college species, but it is very doubtful whether those are any loss. A person who is a born teacher will get his subject across at least as well as the orthodox type who has passed through the mass-production mill of the Ministry of Education.

The Headmaster of Clayesmore, Mr. R. L. Everett, was most kind and generous in every possible way, and I still feel a deep debt of gratitude to this truly Christian man for his unfailing helpfulness to me. His subordinates were equally kind to me. There was, for example, Mr. W. Yorke, the English master, a man who I am sure could never have survived a training college with his unique temperament, but whose rich and many-sided culture was an asset of inestimable value to the school. Like Baroness Orczy's "Old Man in the Corner", he was never seen without a piece of string, and with that piece of string he could perform absolute miracles.

Yorke owned a car, if it could be dignified with that description, of the 1919 vintage. It had four wheels as a rule, plus a steering-wheel, which depended to no small extent upon its owner's string. The chariot should have been named "Faith", or possibly "Hope," but Yorke insisted upon calling it "Eliza". How that contraption ever moved at all was a mystery to the most able of mechanics. But not only did it move, it ran over whole continents with the incomprehensible facility of a magic carpet. Its engine, to all appearances, could scarcely have set a cigar-box in motion. Yet when each vacation came round Yorke would load up his uncomplaining steed with burdens that would have put a strain upon a traction-engine, and all would be tied down with the ubiquitous string. String, in fact, took on an entirely new meaning when you knew Yorke.

Spain was this amazing character's happy hunting ground, as it was later to become mine. From the Pyrenees to the Rock of Gibraltar Yorke's faithful bone-shaker sped its untroubled way. Expensive cars were frequently to be seen standed along the Spanish roadside, but never "Eliza". Across the stony stretches of Andalusia she would grunt and groan, but her heart was wed to Yorke, and never did she let him down. One felt instinctively that no matter for how many more decades she might trundle her noble course, the end would surely come at the conclusion of one of those lengthy pilgrimages through Europe; most certainly not at the beginning of such a journey, and beyond all question not in its middle—not so long as the magic piece of string was forthcoming, anyway.

For Yorke I had a sincere regard. Years later, long after my departure from Clayesmore, I caught a fleeting glimpse of him on a Tangier-bound ferry boat from Gibraltar. Since there was a hundred yards of sea between us, no reunion was possible. But the memories brought to life by that brief sight of my former friend and colleague were extremely happy ones.

Another particularly pleasant personality in the school was Henry Teed, the young maths and handicrafts master. Any school would be glad to claim a man of Teed's calibre. Far too many educational establishments provide little of value to the non-academic type of boy. But at Clayesmore, both in the Senior School and in the Junior, the practical side of education was seriously regarded, and that was where Teed came in. He was, for instance, a perfect genius at boat-building. Each spring a fine, new craft, constructed during the long, dark winter evenings, would be proudly launched upon the nearby river. It would carry perfectly fashioned sails, and no detail essential to scientific sailing would be omitted. Eight boys could board the boat at a time, and the many hours of rich contentment thus afforded them was considered a more than adequate reward for months of toil.

Pottery, too, was a handicraft which occupied a very important place in school life, and this, together with painting, made up a full and healthy programme after lessons were over. The results of both these crafts used to be sold on Speech Day in aid of a fund to purchase equipment for such amenities as table tennis and a variety of hobbies. On Speech Day, also, a play was invariably presented for the entertainment of the parents and other visitors.

A still further very interesting feature of our set-up was the Junior School Assembly, or Parliament. This was not merely a debating society. It was a form of decentralized government, whereby boys could present bills advocating improvements of one sort or another in school life. All such bills were, of course, subject to veto by the Headmaster; but any really sound and sensible proposal would be seriously debated and, provided it did not incur the veto, was incorporated in the school rules and regulations. This training in the exercise of democratic citizenship was a valuable contribution to the communal life and gave the boys a real interest in their school.

Clayesmore was an intensely happy school. The discipline, though good, was free from all oppression, and corporal punishment was a thing almost unknown. A system of plus and minus awards for good or bad conduct determined the enjoyment of privileges or their deprivation. The total was registered on a big chart, and any boy who accumulated more than a certain number of minuses had to appear before a joint meeting of masters and prefects. And here, too, properly democratic principles were observed, for the boys were permitted to plead their case, and judgment was passed by the combined assembly.

The days were full and rewarding, and in this happy atmosphere the wounds of my tragic experience with the Archbishop began to heal. And as time went on and I maintained my serious reading, I discovered more and more sound reasons for returning to the original faith out of which both Christianity and Islam had grown. I retained a profound respect and admiration for Jesus and His followers, and I fully recognized the many praiseworthy episodes in the history of the Church. Beyond, this, however, I could not go. The notion of the Eternal King of the Universe becoming a human baby, beautiful as I felt it to be, was to my thinking outside the bounds of acceptance. The idea of directing any form of worship to a created being, no matter how saintly he or she might have been, became utterly repugnant to me. And as my appreciation of the infinite nature of God developed, so did I find all forms of religion which failed to conform to a strictly monotheistic standard unworthy of credence. Coincidentally with the increasing direction of all my fervour to God Himself, I became aware of a knitting together of my personality, so to speak, and the assumption of an inner unity and power such as I had never previously known.

Nevertheless, I realized that this monotheistic conception by no means represented Judaism in its entirety. My researches had shown me, in fact, that Judaism, while monotheistic in a strict sense of the word, was less a creed than a way of life; every action throughout the livelong day was linked in one way or another to Judaism. If I was to be a Jew I could not merely believe in One God and leave it at that; the Unitarian Church did as much. On the contrary, I would have to live in the manner prescribed for Jews when the Law was given to Moses on Sinai. The Dietary Laws and those concerned with observance of the Sabbath were fundamental. Moreover, it was essential that I be circumcised. My problem, in fact, was only a quarter solved as yet, and the hardest part of its solution was still to come.

I was desperately eager to expedite my reception into the Jewish Community. First and foremost among the features of Judaism which my studies had taught me to admire, I think, was its intense practicality. Thoughts of the world to come were not permitted to distract the Jew from fulfilling as completely as possible his mission here on earth. Jews did not simply sit passive and wait for the Messiah to come, for if they did so He would not come. His coming could only be hastened by *mitzvot*—their own good works. A hymn on the lines of "O Paradise, O Paradise, 'tis weary waiting here" could find no place on a Jewish tongue.

Then there was that splendid, robust principle of assuming undivided personal responsibility for one's actions. I had so often felt that the dual aspect of religious life among Catholics, with devout piety and the commission of mortal sins seeming to share so paradoxical a co-existence, stemmed from their undue reliance on the sacramental system, whereby much personal responsibility to God was either absolved or transferred to others—priests, saints, or the Virgin. Judaism, by contrast, insists that its follower shall give his whole heart, soul, and mind to the Eternal Creator. The Jew must stand upright on his own two feet before the Judge of All. He has no patron saints to plead his cause, no Father Confessor to grant indulgences, absolutions, or dispensations. He is, in the fullest sense, the "master of his fate, the captain of his soul". He neither has, nor asks for, any intermediary to bear his brief before the Judge of Heaven. Each man is his own barrister. He must plead his own cause, with a sincere heart that is truly repentant, to God alone.

Judaism does not and cannot offer any season tickets to Heaven at reduced prices. Every pilgrim travels under his own steam, so to speak. The Jew believes that he, as all men, has sufficient will-power, assisted by prayer, to resist any evil inclination. He does not require an extravagant sacramental system, born of human ingenuity rather than of divine revelation, to snatch him from the fires of God's anger. And a Jew either gives all to God or does not bother with external religion at all. He does not bargain with God for special terms. Whatever his failings may be—and many Jews do fail grievously, it cannot be denied—he at least does not whine about God's asking too much of him. He strikes his breast and confesses, "I have sinned and fallen short." Even on the great Day of Atonement, it is clearly understood, however, that only the sins directly against God are thus forgiven. Sins committed against his neighbour are forgiven only after he has begged his neighbour's forgiveness, and he must, if necessary, ask often. The Catholic Christian, on the other hand, can harm his neighbour, go to Confession, make a sincere act of contrition, and receive forgiveness forthwith. He can still complacently go his way without begging pardon of the injured neighbour.

These and many other outstanding characteristics of

Judaism filled me, as I have said, with eagerness to embrace it with all speed. But it would be two years before my case could even receive serious consideration. True, I had made my final break with the Church, but that was by no means sufficient. The Beth Din—the Central Jewish Authority, literally the "House of Law" of British Jewry—had first to be completely satisfied of my ability to live in a Jewish community. They demanded that I should obtain employment in a Jewish environment, in order to give myself the opportunity of proving that I possessed that ability.

I was in a heart-breaking position. I had left everything behind to enter the Jewish community, yet here I was, compelled to live without its consolations and suspended in a vacuum, as it were, neither Christian nor Jew. However, there was nothing to be done except to make the best of this anomalous situation. Although I was under no obligation at this time to observe the Jewish law, I strained every nerve by way of preparation, to keep as much of the Jewish way of life as my surroundings permitted. Accordingly, without any encouragement from the Beth Din, I attempted to observe the Dietary Laws by eating only vegetarian food. Also, with Scripture lessons on my time-table, I taught exclusively from the Old Testament, and on Saturdays I taught only orally, doing no writing. And when I had to take my turn as church escort for the boys, I sat at the back. But these self-imposed acts of discipline were no more than palliatives for my sense of frustration, my impatience to take the great step.

And so there was no alternative to seeking that fresh employment in a Jewish environment, on which the authorities had insisted, with the least possible delay.

8

More Temptations—Then a Haven

"Licence they mean when they cry Liberty."
JOHN MILTON

"I believe with perfect Faith that the Creator, blessed be his name, knows every deed of the children of Men, and all their thoughts, as it is said: It is He that fashioneth the hearts of them all, that giveth heed to all their deeds."
Article 10 of "13 Articles of Faith", MAIMONIDES. (9)

THERE was, however, some considerable delay before I was able to choose that Jewish environment wherein I had been bidden to subject myself to the test. Finally, the day came when I discovered an environment ideal to the purpose. This was Carmel College, at Newbury, in Berkshire, founded three years earlier—still a century late, however—and sometimes called the "Anglo-Jewish Eton".

I recall so vividly my first visit to the college, on a lovely day in August 1951. As I learned later, it was the day after the birth of little David, the youngest son of Rabbi Kopul Rosen, the Rector. The first sight that met my eyes on entering the grounds was that of the older boy, Jeremy, standing on a chair on the lawn and fervently addressing an imaginary audience. He had inherited his father's great gift of eloquence, plus a good measure of self-assurance. In fact, he was, and still is, a real chip off the old block. Needless to say, the spectacle of the small boy in that rhetorical rôle called back to memory my own childhood practice of sermonizing the long-suffering adult members of our household!

The college appealed to me at first sight. The buildings were set in beautiful rural surroundings, and on that sunny August afternoon I found the peace quite heavenly. I could not help feeling it augured well for my future. And when it came to the fateful interview Dr. Rosen received me most graciously, and his personality, as the saying goes, came out to meet me. Within a matter of seconds I was under the spell of a most dynamic character. All through my life it has seemed that I have been privileged to encounter really outstanding men. Archbishops, scholars, nobility, and other men of influence have enriched my varied experience. But Dr. Rosen was the equal of any of them in force of personality. He took me to his study, discussed terms with me, and made a generous settlement in salary.

Returning to London, my heart sang a hymn of thanksgiving. The Lord had indeed been good to me. He had "led me beside the still waters, made me to lie down in green pastures, and restored my soul". The promised land appeared now to be just around the corner. This, as it turned out, was not quite the case, but God nevertheless was working out His purpose.

I had signed a contract for five years at Clayesmore, and the first step I had to take, of course, was to get my release from this contract. There was a little difficulty at first in obtaining this concession, but in the end Mr. Everett, the Headmaster, with his unfailing generosity, met my request. It was with genuine regret, though, that I took my leave of Clayesmore. The boys, too, I could see, were upset. They asked to be allowed to keep in touch with me, and of course I welcomed their suggestion, though I realized that in the circumstances it was unlikely to be fulfilled. I had to content myself with the knowledge that I had done my best for them, and that in return I had been privileged to receive their trust, love, and gratitude. This was a great consolation to me in the trials that were still to come.

But there now arose a very serious problem—the recurrent one of finance. My new post at Carmel College would not officially begin until October, and this meant that I must support myself for three months. Had I mentioned the fact to Dr. Rosen, I have not the slightest doubt that the openhanded Rector would have taken steps to cover my needs. But I had never believed in straining any person's goodwill. There was too little generosity in this hard world, and I was of no mind to abuse such as there was.

I determined, therefore, to do again what I and thousands

of others had done as students during the early days of the War; to get a job to tide me over. I had then been temporarily employed in the Ministry of Food headquarters. A young Jewish medical student and I had been given the task of zoning the fish supplies. The fish, however, being apparently fifth columnists, had refused to co-operate, resolutely declining to oblige the Ministry by being zoned. They swam their own selfish ways, leaving the country to divide its sea-food to the best of its ability. As my colleague expressed it with an atrocious pun, the transport at our disposal consequently had to convey the fish "from plaice to place". With a little voluntary distribution along the coastline, things might have been so much easier.

This time, however, I could not claim the privileges of a student and there was no war. A humbler status, therefore, was indicated. What I really needed was a good holiday, but in my reduced circumstances that would have to wait. So I went to one of the largest catering concerns in the country and, on the strength of my wartime employment in the Ministry of Food, was taken on as a kitchen hand. It was warm work, and it left me in a perpetual bath of sweat. But the concern was a sweat-shop in another sense, too. It was, alas, owned by Jews; and as in so many other cases, the owners, who were so notable for kindness in other respects, had no consideration at all for their employees in business. It is mainly in business that far too many people still relapse into the outlook of jungle warfare. Jews, being a minority, would be well advised to meditate upon the ultimate repercussions of this policy. It breeds anti-Semitism, and in the final issue it nurtures Communism. Although by no means a Socialist, I have often felt that if I were in power one of the first things I would do would be to nationalize all catering concerns.

I found lodgings near the restaurant where I worked, and there I lived, as I had done at Clayesmore, on vegetables and fruit. I was highly conscious, needless to say, of the paradox in a situation in which I, not yet a Jew, was straining every nerve to adhere to Jewish laws, while everywhere I saw those born as Jews happily stuffing themselves with ham sandwiches. Either I was crazy, I concluded, or else they were the last word in perversity. Why should I, who had yet to be received into Judaism, stand on my head to keep dietary laws which 70 per cent of Jewry dismissed with contempt? It called for a will of iron to hold my course. If only I could have felt at least a minimum of moral support. But no, I was to be tested as gold in the furnace, right up to the last moment and beyond.

Neither was the social atmosphere of my working surroundings, I regret to say, calculated to assist me in my strivings for a new way of life. The men and women with whom I was brought in contact were friendly and pleasant enough, but their lives were utterly devoid of any spiritual or moral horizons. They ate, drank, fornicated, and slept. Rising each morning, they simply repeated the routine—eating, drinking, promiscuity, and sleep. And thus their animal existences went on, day after day and week after week without end.

To cut myself off entirely from my workmates was clearly impossible. Nor was it altogether desirable that I should do so, for this was a unique opportunity for me to gain experience of how the other half of the world lived. On several occasions I accepted invitations from some of the fellows to go out with them for a drink in the evenings. A number of them, married men included, would pick up girls and spend the remainder of the evening in their company. I preferred, however, to stay with the stag section of the party, and thus avoid unnecessary complications; and the young married men, realizing perhaps that their type of amusement did not fit in with my ideas, did not press me to follow their example. And of this I am glad. I had no wish to offend them, but the affair with Martin in Soho had been my first experience of its kind, and I was determined that it should be my last. It had been only in my distraught condition, and out of a desire for revenge rather than of a craving of the flesh, that I had courted danger. It had struck a note quite foreign to my nature and harshly out of tune with my whole being.

I felt great regret at the way these young fellows were throwing away their marriages, but there was nothing I could do about it, nor was it any of my affair. After all, they were old enough to know their own minds. Several among their number, sensing no doubt a sympathetic disposition, had confided to me their boredom at home, frequently the result of the constant nagging they received from wives who had lost their power to charm and attract. After a hard day's work, they would tell me, they felt quite unable to go home and face this ordeal. So instead they made the time-worn excuses about working late and sought the company of girls who still felt an inclination to please them and give them the complete satisfaction they desired. This flattered their vanity as well as supplying them with the feminine sympathy for which they craved so desperately.

Their stories taught me to understand what grave risks are run by indifferent or offhand wives. There are always plenty of unattached girls only too anxious to entertain other people's husbands. Nor does it greatly worry the majority of these women if they are told the truth about their lovers' marital status or discover it for themselves. It is apt, in fact, to add a certain extra relish to their conquests.

About half-way through my period of employment, one of the women working in the restaurant, much older than I was and separated from her husband, developed a strong "crush" on me. She did her utmost during business hours to foster an intimate relationship, and on frequent occasions she invited me to her house. I always managed to refuse these on one pretext or another, but each time it grew more difficult to find an adequate excuse. On the occasion of her birthday—and I should guess it marked well over the half-century for her—she issued an invitation to the entire staff to attend a party, and everybody accepted. This naturally placed me in a very embarrassing position, since strictly speaking she was my "superior officer" who normally gave me all my orders. Moreover, my fellow workers made it clear that they took a distinctly dim view of my intended refusal. So in these difficult circumstances I decided it would be wise to attend.

That night the drinks flowed fast and freely, and the women showed themselves even faster and more free. Our hostess' four rooms, including the bathroom, were given up to love-making in the strictest biological interpretation of the term. For the first part of the evening I contrived somehow to avoid my potential source of danger. After supper, however, under the pretence of getting me to help her wipe the dishes, she inveigled me into the kitchen. The others, in response to a broad hint, took themselves elsewhere, visibly amused at my predicament. After all, my hostess' presumable plans for me were completely in keeping with the general atmosphere of the party. Everybody was full of drink, the air was thick and heady. In every corner marriage-vows were being thrown out of the window. Young men, some of them married only a year or two, were behaving like the least responsible of wild bachelors.

Left alone in the kitchenette with this desperate, love-starved woman, I was facing a real test. One thing I knew beyond all doubt; I was not going to succumb to her wiles. At the first possible opportunity I would plead a headache and beat a retreat. But just as I registered this firm resolve, the lady, without the slightest warning, threw her arms around me and held me to her in a bear-like grip. Why did I avoid her? she demanded. After all, she went on, I was so lonely and so much in need of waking up, and she could give me such a good time! Terrified out of my wits and wondering helplessly what to do, I stood rooted there as though bound hand and foot. I was bewildered by the atmosphere, the dread of creating a scene, and the apparent hopelessness of my situation. On a sudden impulse I hugged my companion in return and kissed her.

How much longer frail human nature could have held out must always remain uncertain, for at this very critical juncture there came a sudden diversion which came to my rescue. One of the young men, in his unsteady condition, had blundered against our hostess' china cupboard, smashing the glass and several of her cherished ornaments. She was furious, and her language made the most foul-mouthed of the men's cherubic choirboys by comparison. She stormed and cursed and threw everything she could lay her hands on at the unhappy culprit. Vows were cheap, but china precious! We passed round the hat and collected about five pounds which would cover the damage and leave something over to soothe her outraged feelings. And thus the delicate situation was retrieved.

It was 3 a.m. when the party broke up. The married men had presumably pleaded "night shift" as their alibi; for cleaning shifts did come round regularly, and provided the excuse was not produced too often, the truant husband stood a good chance of avoiding detection. Some, it must be understood, cared little and were hoping, in fact, that their wives would divorce them. Such, at all events, was the spectacle which presented itself to the priest-turned-kitchen-hand. Hearing confessions in a church and actually witnessing sinners in action, especially as one of their own class, were two entirely different things. Yet I had to admit to myself that the change was a welcome and refreshing one—at all events for a limited period of time!

The lady of the house urgently pressed me to stay the night. She implored me not to leave her in her present condition. Some of my colleagues, too, joined in the supplication, whispering to me that I would be a bloody fool to miss such a heaven-sent opportunity. No harm could come of it at her age, they pointed out, and they would keep their mouths shut at work about it. Not, of course, that anybody would think any the less of me for getting experience; just the contrary in fact, but still . . . Others, on the other hand, advised me to look for something better. However, I was not torn between conflicting impulses. My own feelings left me in no doubt whatsoever. Nothing, I now knew, could prevail upon me to fall into such a trap, however attractive might be the bait. Calming my would-be mistress, therefore, with a last passionate kiss, I left the house and hastened off in the direction of my lodgings.

Reaction had set in by this time, and I felt nauseated as I had never felt before. That night I had met humanity at rock-bottom. I had allowed myself to flirt with perilous things which it had always been my instinct to keep at arm's length. True, the experience was one which I could not feel too sorry to have had, with its forceful object-lesson in the uglier facts of life, but it was the end. No matter how many weeks of my bondage remained to be endured, from now on I would conduct myself simply as a good-natured workmate. There could be no more social relationships. Snob or no snob, I had a worthwhile future to preserve, and I could not, and would not, permit myself to be cheated out of it. For otherwise my renunciation would amount to nothing more than spiritual suicide. I knew now something of how the other half of the world lived, and I wished to content myself with that bit of knowledge. Agreeable as these people might be, they were of a different breed. Figuratively they spoke a different language and inhabited a world which for me was quite meaningless.

That early morning I did not bother to go to bed. I simply took a bath, changed my suit, and prayed as perhaps I had never prayed before. Even as a priest I had often used my own extemporised prayers in addition to the breviary, and I did so now. By breakfast-time I had, I felt, cleansed my mind and heart of the bad taste left by the events of the previous night. I felt clean once more, both within and without.

Back at work, however, new problems awaited me. Some of my fellow workers, wrongly interpreting my presence and behaviour at the party as indicating an adoption of their way of life, went out of their way to be particularly friendly. Their former reserve had given place to an attitude of chumminess. They teased me about my "narrow escape" and tried to egg me on to embark on a regular affair with someone more worth my while. Though takings pains not to offend them, I used the excuse provided by my language classes, which were due to begin that week, to avoid going out with them. And as for my *inamorata* I visited her no more, though she was obviously upset by my defection.

How it would all have ended had I remained, I cannot say; but fortunately Providence, usually to be relied upon to support those who fight temptation, stepped in at this juncture. Its intervention took the form of a transfer to another branch, where the majority of the temporary staff were students. With these I had much in common, and my final spell of work was therefore pleasant and congenial. I waited impatiently for October to come, bringing the commencement of my job at Carmel College. Meanwhile I continued with my study of Judaism in all its aspects, and as my researches progressed I experienced an ever-increasing satisfaction within. Any troubles from now onwards would be merely on the surface. No longer would my mind and heart be torn asunder by conflict.

As was, of course, only to be expected, people and circumstances frequently irritated me, even in this so much more agreeable sphere of work. But these were just the pin-pricks inevitable in any environment; for since most of our troubles are from within, and we take ourselves with us everywhere, we can never be entirely free from problems. Of one thing I was quite certain; I had attained an internal wholeness and unity which no surface storms and trials could destroy.

The strongest adverse emotion I now experienced, and was still often to experience again even at Carmel, was that caused by naturally powerful currents of nostalgia. I hope I have made it clear that my self-severance from the Roman Church implied no quarrel with Catholicism as such. Far from it, indeed. True, there had been some frictions involved, but these had stemmed purely from personal incompatibilities. My sole reason for parting from the Church had been my utter inability to accept any longer a number of its dogmas and my unwillingness to play the hypocrite by feigning to accept them. Coupled with this was the irresistible pull exerted upon me by what I felt to be the simple, fundamental truths of the Old Faith.

It would indeed have been strange if, after years of active ministry among people whom I had deeply loved, memories did not from time to time tug at my heart-strings. I had not left my state of life for any dissatisfaction with my flock. The external work of the priesthood had, right up to the last, afforded me the deepest satisfaction. The Archbishop had gone to his rest, and his successor might well have taken a kindlier view of my activities. The pulpit, too, had always attracted me, and youth work, especially with the influence and prestige of the priesthood behind me, had been satisfying beyond all description. So it was scarcely to be wondered at if at times scenes of my full and fruitful labours came flooding into my memory, tinged with a sense of loss. This tendency might have constituted a danger, but it failed to do so. Within minutes the nostalgia storm would blow over and my disposition to regret would dissolve as though it had never been.

At long last came October, and with it my move to Carmel College. This was a joyful occasion to me, and a proud one. Although at that time it had only been going for three years, the College had two hundred pupils and already had an academic record to be proud of. It has since added further to its honours by pupils gaining an open scholarship to Balliol College, Oxford, and State scholarships to both Oxford and Cambridge. And its extra-scholastic triumphs, too, have been worthy of note. Recently a Carmel team went to Eton for the final round of an inter-Public School chess competition and won it by 4 games to 2.

But Carmel's most outstanding successes have been moral and social. Boys who had proved beyond the powers of psychiatrists have, within months, settled down to a normal life. There is something therapeutic about the school's whole atmosphere. A boy is tolerated in his idiosyncracies and even excesses, though not to the extent of permitting him to endanger others. It is he, and not they, who change. Boys of extremely nervous and temperamental disposition are soothed and strengthened within the moderate and moderating discipline of the school.

In the religious sphere, too, Carmel has its successes to record, and in its benign atmosphere many boys who came from irreligious Jewish homes which cared little for Judaism, have found the way back to the faith of their fathers. The spiritual life at Carmel is neither fanatically religious nor loosely Liberal. It is traditional and Orthodox in both belief and practice. In a word, it represents the Judaism of the Torah, the Eternal's code for His people. The school, transferred four years ago to Mongewell Park, near Wallingford, Berkshire, certainly deserves all the material support that it can possibly get.

Of Dr. Rosen, the Rector of Carmel, I have already related how dynamic a personality I felt him to be at our very first interview, and as time went on and I grew to know him better, I found no reason to amend my initial impression. It is no exaggeration to say that Dr. Rosen's personality dominated the atmosphere at Carmel as the Empire State Building dominates the New York skyline. So far as force of character went, I have not the slightest doubt that he could have become an important factor in the political life of Israel had he so desired. He was vital, modern in approach, versatile, more courageous than a lion, and the finest orator to be found anywhere in Britain. The problems, crises, and communal onslaughts which he suffered during the first seven years of his work in building Carmel would have finished off most men not in possession of similar toughness.

If this great man had a weakness it was that his early struggles and frustrations had left him, as was but natural, liable to occasional spells of moodiness. But the clouds invariably passed, and with their passing the sun shone forth again in all its glory. I came to picture the Rector in my imagination as a reincarnation of King Saul. And Dr. Rosen, like Saul, had a David to soothe him and chase away black moods when they threatened to descend, for David Stamler, at present vice-rector, made it his special mission to be that David. And the Rector—unlike Saul in this, however—was loyal to his David. Our friendship has remained unimpaired through the years, and I feel I cannot sum it up better than by saying that when I meditated upon his courage and generosity I realized that, in spite of my unusually rich experience of great men, I had never met Dr. Rosen's superior.

My first year at Carmel was to prove a most strenuous one. Although, unfortunately, circumstances had made it impossible for me to prepare myself for it by taking a holiday, I thoroughly enjoyed my new environment and found complete satisfaction in its varied duties. I was appointed to teach in the Senior School during the day, and to act as Housemaster in the Preparatory School, which was situated three miles away, at night. Any stress and strain that I may have felt was undoubtedly due to my having gone so long without any sort of vacation; and taking that into consideration, I considered that I was standing very well up to the ordeal.

The Master-in-charge of the Preparatory School was a Mr. Toffman, and he was the *beau idéal* of the sergeant-major type —walrus moustache, parade-ground bellow, lively and pungent wit, and all the rest of the traditional characteristics. As an organizer and disciplinarian he was superb, though a little more rough-and-ready perhaps, than the polished types normally to be found occupying the tutelary position he did. That, however, was wholly in keeping with the general character of the Preparatory School staff, which was altogether unlike that of the normal scholastic kind. Take, for example, the Resident Housemaster, Dr. Rurely, who came from Beersheba, Israel. He was a charming, gentle soul if ever there was one, but there were two things he seemed to hate as the Devil is said to hate holy water: namely, good order and discipline. The latter he despised with a fanatical loathing. According to his view, a boy must be completely uninhibited. The walls and ceiling might collapse, every pane of glass disintegrate into minutest fragments, but the boy must not be in any way suppressed.

I myself had other ideas on the subject of discipline. Indeed, during my early days many a spoiled mother's darling made an intimate acquaintance with my slipper. After a while it became no longer necessary to perform the rôle of executioner, but the total lack of discipline as I had found it on my arrival had been beyond all sufferance. Jewish boys, I was rapidly discovering, were charming, full of personality, and generous to a fault, but—and it was a big "but"—they were terribly spoiled by their doting parents. There seemed to be an unwritten law that a Jewish father or mother denied their child nothing within their power to give.

When the boys arrived at school, accompanied to the very doors in many cases by their worshipping parents, it was a positive revelation. I tried to picture such scenes taking place at Clayesmore, or at any other Public School for that matter, but it was beyond the scope of imagination. One big-hearted and ample-bosomed mother, a Mrs. Roginson, cornered me one day at the head of the stairs.

"Ah, there you are, Mr. Carmel," she exclaimed. "I've been looking for you for two hours."

I knew only too well why she had been looking and, just because I did, I had been hiding from her. But the beginning of Term Assembly in the hall demanded my presence; and so, emerging stealthily from my den, I had hoped to reach the rostrum undetected. But no such luck: Mrs. Roginson was an experienced hand in the art of waylaying shy masters.

There was no escape except by the unthinkable expedient of taking a flying leap over the banisters. I had to see it through, though while doing so I edged slowly but surely away, keeping one eye ingratiatingly on the anxious mother and the other on my watch. If I could only manage one step per second, I figured, I might still get away in time for Roll Call.

"I was saying to my husband," Mrs. Roginson continued —and I saw that gentleman peeping nervously from behind the commanding figure of his wife—"I was saying that Monty simply must have a rubber-foam mattress. Would you see to that, please, Mr. Carmel?"

"Well, you know, Mrs. Roginson," I pointed out in reply, "those rubber mattresses are only for the boys who are taken ill."

"Yes, yes, my dear Mr. Carmel," the lady persisted, inexorably keeping step with my attempted edging away, "but you know what it is for a new boy just away from home! We'll send his electric blanket in November, and his nylon undies as well."

I thought this would conclude the parental attack, but worse was yet to come.

"By the way, Mr. Carmel," came the next phase of the offensive, "could we send in some chicken for Monty—twice a week, say? He does so love his food, you know!"

At this, however, I felt that I really had to take a firm line.

"No, no, Mrs. Roginson, I'm afraid that is quite out of the question," I answered. "Dr. Rosen does not permit gift parcels."

"Oh, well," my persecutor gushed, "in that case I'll just drop a line to Dr. Rosen. He was at *Yeshiva* * with my sister's husband in Capolski. That was a few years ago, of course, but they were just like brothers—fought all day long! As my dear mother used to say—rest her soul!—she always knew Kopul Rosen would become a great headmaster. Such

* College for Hebrew studies.

brains, my dear, and what an orator! Licks spots off the Rabbi at our *stibel*,* I assure you! Nice little fellow and all that, you know, but the Rabbi can't preach for toffee. You know, of course, Mr. Carmel, that my hubby gives a lot of money to that *stibel*. No appeal ever goes out but what Rudy gives a cool thousand. Isn't that so, Rudy?"—Here the timid husband advanced a step and nodded modestly—"Oh, Dr. Rosen will let Monty have his rubber mattress and his chicken twice a week; you just see if he doesn't!"

At this point, fortunately, who should come on the scene but Dr. Rosen himself, and he hastened to my rescue.

"Well, now, I was just saying, Dr. Rosen," Mrs. Roginson resumed, turning her batteries on the Rector, but he cut her short without ceremony.

"Yes, yes, Mrs. Roginson," he beamed, "you want Monty to have chicken twice a week, and three rubber mattresses a month! When he gets home in December he'll need them all, I'm sure, but meantime the bell is just about to ring, and I shouldn't like you to be swept away by a hundred young savages charging downstairs! Don't worry, Mrs. Roginson, we'll make a civilized human being out of your brat!"

At that, Mrs. Roginson, discomfited, routed, bereft of words possibly for the first time in her loquacious life, and also a little fearful, too, of the threatened avalanche down the stairs, retreated with her Rudy in tow. Dr. Rosen's masterly handling of the situation fascinated me.

So long as the Rector was at the Preparatory School Assembly, order and awe prevailed. Then, when after a few words of welcome to the visitors he returned to the Senior School, the Assembly was taken over by Dr. Rurely. No sooner had the latter ascended the rostrum, whistle in hand, than the air was rent by a hundred screaming voices. Dr. Purley might just as well have been back in Beersheba. The louder he blew his whistle, the higher rose the shrill voices of the invading army of Hebrew warriors in short pants. But

* Small synagogue.

just when it seemed inevitable that the Assembly would break up in chaos, the Master-in-charge, Mr. Hoffman, arrived on the scene. At his barrack-square roar the din of battle died away. Twitching his handle-bar moustache ferociously, Toffman eyed the insurgents and gorgonized them with his stony glare. And then, in true sergeant-major style, he told them their fortunes. They learned more about their small selves from him in five minutes than they had heard in all the twelve years of their previous existence.

Yes, this was indeed a strange world I had come into. But I loved it.

9

Continued Delay

"There is society where none intrudes."
Childe Harold, BYRON

"Which is a small verse upon which all the principles of Torah are dependant? 'In all thy ways acknowledge Him' (Prov. 3, 6), which means that in all your actions . . . you must acknowledge the Lord and do them for the sake of His name, blessed be He."
Code of Jewish Law, Book 1, Chapter 31.1. (10)

WITH every day that I spent at Carmel, I came to realize more and more clearly how essential it is for a teacher to have a true vocation for such work. No one can engage satisfactorily in the sphere of education unless he is dedicated, heart, mind, and soul, to his vital task. The real objective of an educator is the formation of character of his pupil no less than providing the information of his mind. In a boarding school especially, those entrusted with the work must have a genuine call. There must be no half-measures and no trade-union mentality. The needs of the pupils, whether they be urgent or merely trivial, cannot be met by those whose eyes are upon the clock or who take little interest in the lives of their young charges.

During the last war large numbers of men were rushed through our teachers' training in England regardless of their real suitability. Where I myself was concerned, on the other hand, I have often reflected that I started out with a distinct advantage on my side: namely, that in leaving behind the bustle and activity of the ministry in order to engage in scholastic work, I was following, though perhaps unconsciously, a tradition which was by no means strange or new in the history of English education. For until fairly recently the headmasters of most English Public Schools were ordained clergymen. The two vocations have much in common; a "call" is essential in both spheres, and much damage is done when either a schoolmaster or a clergyman is a mere career man.

The point I am endeavouring to make is this. I am fully

persuaded that my previous experience as a priest, and especially in youth work, was of material help to me in fully realizing what it means to children at boarding school to be deprived of the natural affection which their parents alone can adequately give. If those who stand in the place of parents have no genuine regard for the children, then indeed the loss is tragic and irreparable. A good boy will always miss a good home, and he must be able to feel that a strong but kindly hand continues to attend to his problems and crises. Some people prefer to let boys grow without attention like grass in a field. This can be a dangerous policy, if not a criminal one, and is every bit as bad as spoiling them.

Particularly vital is the function of the housemaster. He must know his boys thoroughly and be able always to recognize the appropriate moment to apply either pressure or relief. Some masters suffer from difficulties which arise from the nature of their pupils' home environment. Unless the educator enjoys the full co-operation of the parent he is swimming against a strong tide. Parents who spoil their sons at home, like the egregious Mrs. Roginson, defeat the whole purpose which their sacrifice in sending their sons to a good school ought to achieve.

Teaching demands both a distinterested zeal and a great deal of faith. Boys are by nature apt to be selfish. I need not enter at any length into the psychological reasons for this, apart from observing in passing that it is concerned mainly with the boys' realization of their growing powers and their struggle to establish themselves in a new society. It is a great mistake for those engaged in educational work to identify themselves too closely with those they teach. They must be genuinely interested, of course, but it must be without hope of reward or recognition. A few grateful natures will show appreciation, but such boys are in the minority and, as a rule, mature beyond their years. Most boys are of a self-centred species who will wag their tails so long as you please them, but are equally ready to snarl or bite should you offend them. They will remember a single punishment while forgetting many acts of kindness.

The building of character is the most vital of all work from every point of view, but it must be its own reward. One day, perhaps, when it is too late, our democracies will appreciate the truth. A teacher is infinitely more important to the future life of a country than, for example, a bus-conductor or truck-driver, but it is the latter who stand the better chance of earning adequate remuneration. A headmistress with a degree will frequently command less than the truck-driver; and as for an assistant master or mistress, their pay is less than that of many a skilled labourer. When we consider that the moulding of the future generation is so largely in the hands of educators, we are forced to realize how short-sighted is the policy of our Departments of Education.

There are many people who look upon schoolmasters as a queer race of beings, and it must be admitted that some of the breed do appear to be somewhat abnormal. This, no doubt, is especially true in the case of bachelors, particularly those who have spent their whole lives within the narrow confines of one or two educational centres. On the other hand, I believe it is true to say that when a great many men look back over their lives it is to their schooldays and their schoolmasters to whom their thoughts return with special affection and gratitude. I have in the course of my life met many famous men and listened to their words, but it is the sayings of my schoolmasters that I constantly remember throughout the years. How often, for example, has that dictum of my schoolmaster when I was ten years old, "Aim at the stars and nothing lower," come to my assistance when some difficult task lay before me! For long after ordinary lessons have been forgotten—if, indeed, they were ever learned—an inspiring injunction such as that, or even some chance remark or piece of kindly advice, will linger for years in the memory. So often it is not what we are paid to teach that helps a boy the most, but rather what comes spontaneously from the heart.

The chief danger in the teaching profession rests, I believe, in the very restricted nature of the teacher's world. He becomes apt to believe that the salvation of mankind may stand or fall upon the strength of a grammatical construction or a geometrical problem's solution. A good teacher has to have a sense of humour strong enough to enable him to laugh at both himself and his material. Once he allows himself to become too intense, he is paving the way, if not to a mental breakdown, at least to an unbalanced life. And another factor indispensable to the good teacher is travel. Every encouragement, in fact, and even help to the point of subsidy, should be given to teachers to spend vacations abroad. They can then say, "I saw so-and-so," and not merely, "In the book it says this and that." It makes just all the difference. And finally, a teacher must also have a hobby or other interest outside his main sphere if he is to keep fresh and effective in his teaching.

One of the chief criticisms I have against the scholastic profession, now that I have had several years of experience in it, is the seeming reluctance of so many teachers to take "refresher" courses in their own or other subjects. Doctors and clergymen frequently meet in conference to discuss their problems, compare notes, and seek solutions. But rarely do members of the teaching profession come together in this way, and the fruit of much valuable experience is lost.

I cannot help feeling, too, that there has also been an undue neglect on the part of the rank-and-file of the teaching profession to acquaint themselves with the newest of the sciences: namely, psychology. Old and outworn methods are tenaciously followed year after year, whether it be from obstinacy or mere conservatism. The mind, the most wonderful of all mechanisms in creation, is less known to us than any other instrument. The medical profession has readily acknowledged the important place which psychology must take in the healing of their patients. It is a matter of positive duty for us to permit it to play its rightful part in the building of the mind and the formation of the character.

Such, then, are some of the conclusions which had begun to take shape in my thoughts during my days at Clayesmore, and which now crystallized with my more extensive experience at Carmel. And Carmel, I may say, presented a most fascinatingly varied field of study. I have tried to describe, for example, the amazing scene of near-riot at the Preparatory School Assembly, and in the Senior School next morning, when I went to teach there, I witnessed an entirely different but no less astonishing performance. Toffman, of the handle-bar moustache and barrack-square manner—incidentally he was a Christian and had come to Carmel from one of the older-established Public Schools—was presiding with rigid but dignified demeanour. His words were clean-cut and rang with a frosty crispness, and the announcement I heard him make was certainly one of the most remarkable I have ever been privileged to hear.

"At precisely seven and a half minutes past nine," he barked, "you will proceed form by form to your form-rooms. At nine twelve point five you will gather your books and stand in the aisles between the desks with your feet eight inches apart. At nine seventeen your Form Masters will enter the form-rooms, and they will at this precise moment proceed to call your names. By nine twenty-three all relevant data will have been duly collected, and you will then have your first lesson, which will be lesson Number Two on the time-table."

Here the fiery martinet paused to cast a baleful eye over his audience to make sure he had their full attention.

"After the break," he continued, "there will be fire-drill. Every boy will go to his dormitory by way of one of three routes. Those boys who are resident on the top floor will go by the back staircase, and those on the first floor by way of the central stairway. You will lie on your beds with your dressing-gowns over you while awaiting the sounding of the alarm. The bottom of the dressing-gown should cover approximately one-third of your ankle, and you should breathe regularly at the rate of two hundred per minute. . . . Now, does any boy not clearly understand?"

Since no one volunteered for further elucidation of these Orders of the Day, the operations were duly carried out, whereupon Hoffman announced that the evacuation of the entire school had taken 2·7 minutes, or five seconds less than in the previous term's exercise. Hoffman's meticulous precision might lead some people to criticize, but it must be borne in mind that his methods, of course, represented the best possible approach to a Hebrew community of any kind. Lack of organization seems the special privilege of Jewish groups, and punctuality seems to rank almost as a mortal sin. All the best Jews, in fact, seem frequently late for an appointment. Whenever I went along to the Court of Ecclesiastical Judges in connection with my application for acceptance into the Jewish faith, I always took two books with me, and as a rule I finished reading them both before gaining admission to the sanctum.

Hoffman's success was the yard-stick of his worth, and his success was impressive. He was in charge of tuition in science. Like most chemists, he tended to be rather circumscribed in outlook, but he was a really fine instructor and always attained his objectives. No boy on the science side ever failed in his examinations. The first six scholarships to Oxford won by Carmel were in science, two of them being open scholarships. Hoffman worked on the assumption that any boy taking an "O"-level paper should work a scholarship course, and to his scholarship candidates he gave degree-papers. The science side boys worked like galley-slaves, burning the midnight oil five nights a week.

Another very distinctive personality was that of the head of the Arts Department, a long, lanky, and leisurely classical scholar from Cambridge named Patrick Warner, who is now in Ethiopia. Like Toffman, he was a Gentile, but unlike

Toffman he was also a philosopher. He shared with his Hebrew colleagues a hearty dislike for clocks and routine, and his attitude towards boys was that they were a pest, but had to be tolerated in a kindly, understanding sort of way.

Warner was to be my departmental chief. My first sight of him was on an occasion in the Staff Common Room when he was engaged in conversation with Roberts, a grand old man of the scholastic world who had emerged from retirement to assist at Carmel in those critical early years. A Welsh Nonconformist, Roberts was a man of firm and noble principles. His mere presence in the school was in itself an invaluable asset, quite apart from his devoted teaching.

"You know, Warner," I heard Roberts saying, "I once taught at a school where there was one Jewish boy—only one, mark you, but ever such a nice boy." He paused to roll one of the home-made cigarettes which were the pride of his life. "Well," he went on, "one day I was teaching either Roman or Greek history, I forget which. Anyway, we had been dealing with empires, and at the end of the lesson this delightful young chap came up to me and said, 'Sir, my father has an empire.' 'Your father has an empire? What on earth do you mean, boy?' I asked him. Well, Warner, what do you think he answered? It turned out he meant that his father owned a huge *emporium* in Guildford or somewhere!"

"Bless my soul!" Warner exclaimed. "In my opinion, Roberts, boys are no more or less than an infernal nuisance. Put 'em in the library, I say, and let 'em read. Far better than all these stupid lessons, where they don't learn a thing!"

And with that Warner straightened himself out to his full six feet four inches and strode out of the room to engage in classical warfare with some boy. For all his talk, he was a most indefatigable and painstaking teacher. No trouble was too much for him to take, and the boys, who were spoon-fed all the way from the Second to the Sixth Form, could command the personal time and attention of this departmental head almost at will. Warner was frequently to be seen coaching some boy, practically a complete stranger to Latin, for a university entrance examination only a bare month ahead.

The staff also included a most fascinating character from Galilee, living today in the United States. Nobody ever used his full name, a matter of at least twenty letters, and we all called him "Skerry" for short. Like so many Israelis, Skerry was a born politician. Notwithstanding a singularly warm and generous nature, his greatest delight was the dangerous amusement of creating situations within the community. He was a great cat-lover. His room was a regular stray cats' home, and we, his colleagues, used to fancy that from his perpetual association with felines he was gradually developing both the outward features and the inward characteristics of that testy species. However that may have been, Sherry, having touched off a first-class row, would purr very much in the manner of the innumerable pussy-cats he had taken under his protection. And when challenged about his intriguings, he would display a broad, disarming grin that melted your wrath as the sun dissolves butter. With a wave of the hand he would simply utter the magic formula "Nah, nah!" which was his final dismissal of all accusations.

Perennially in the wars, too, was Dr. Antonius London, or Toby, as he soon came to be affectionately called by boys and staff alike. Toby was, and still is, the authority *par excellence* on all matters relating to the Calendar. Indeed, even the authorities at Greenwich constantly consult him. He was formerly in the Jewish ministry, but unfortunately suffered a nervous breakdown some years ago, and following a trip to America he took up teaching with a post at Carmel.

I have always felt that this lovable character seems to have somehow missed having any period of adolescence. One gathers that he embarked upon his studies of Plato, Maimonides, and the like in his very cradle. Thanks to this precocious start, what should have been his youthful exuberance had a delayed action which found its outlet only when he came to Carmel, where his perpetual and vivacious polemics, though at first a cause of some anxiety, speedily became a delight to everybody.

Nothing was too trivial to set Lony, on the war-path. Should a colleague or prefect inadvertently omit to respond to his morning greeting, his verbal artillery opened up on the instant with, "Very well! I quite understand I'm not good enough for you to speak to me!" or some such devastating barrage. Peace having at length been signed, the bellicose pedagogue would remain quiescent for a week or so. But then his careful look-out will invariably find a new target, and again the guns will loose their thunder. If a day comes when Toby gets married or is offered a university post the Common Room at Carmel will become very dull and drab.

In an establishment such as Carmel, with such varied types among the staff and ruled over by a headmaster of Dr. Rosen's exceptional force of character, it was inevitable that occasional instances of disagreement should occur between the dynamic Rector and certain of his subordinates. But another of Dr. Rosen's outstanding traits was magnanimity, and after any such incident he would, to all appearances, forget that it had ever happened. It became clear to me from watching several such occasions that he indeed possessed a depth of religious faith to equal his learning and his prominent position in Jewry, and that this was the key to the entire situation.

I could go on writing at length about Carmel and its most noteworthy personalities, but I must return to my own peculiar problems. I had by now been going back and forth to the Jewish Ecclesiastical Judges for a matter of years, and the only visible sign of progress in my case seemed to be that those august authorities no longer snapped my head off as in the early days. But however sharp and lacking in common courtesy some of them might occasionally have appeared to be, I had never for one moment doubted their sincerity, integrity, and lofty ideals. They were veritable pillars of justice—possibly somewhat rough-hewn and narrow in outlook, but none the less a body of men whose uprightness shone clearly through their every word and action. So I continued steadfastly to believe that sooner or later would come the great day when I would learn that my application for reception into Judaism was officially accepted.

Meanwhile, however, it was being made all too clear to me in my personal environment that I was still looked upon as an outsider, if not actually a trespasser. I felt very awkward when the members of the Jewish group of masters huddled into a corner to discuss in lowered voices everything under the sun. Since I was often the only person present who was not in that group, I found myself wondering why they should always go into a conclave to talk over their interests, which presumably should have been my interests also. In retrospect, however, I could not accuse them of any positively uncharitable intention, though they certainly showed themselves thoughtless and inconsiderate.

There was something of a paradox in the situation. As a Christian priest I had found people easy to get on with, but the religion incompatible with my views. As a Jew, on the other hand, I was finding the religion second nature, but its adherents extremely difficult. Yet this in no way detracted from my affection for them. I kept telling myself that even as they appeared harsh to me, so I, for my part, must be proving an embarrassment to them. To reach a satisfactory mutual adjustment would, I saw, require a good deal of give and take. And to show my own sensitiveness would undoubtedly aggravate the situation and give rise to false rumours that I was unsettled.

There is nothing new, of course, in such an experience befalling a convert. A star example is provided by the case of Cardinal Newman, who found himself in a very similar position in the Roman Church. He felt the harshness of older, lifelong Catholics who, having suffered persecution for centuries, had no mercy to spare on the susceptibilities of such a student and of his somewhat weird personality. Whenever Newman was driven to express, even in the most guarded fashion, any hint of anxiety or personal hurt, the gossips eagerly circulated news of his imminent departure from the Church. Such rumours, needless to say, were quite without foundation, but they pained Newman none the less. His fellow convert Manning, on the other hand, who was as tough as nails, survived the communal climate with ease and almost despised Newman for feeling aggrieved.

Bearing in mind, then, that there was nothing unique in my present situation, I decided that it was entirely a matter of settling down to a new existence, getting along with a race of people who were extremely highly strung and emotional, and adapting myself to a completely different outlook on life. The Jewish way of life, self-disciplined as it must of necessity be, presented no hardship to me. It all seemed so reasonable and conducive to union with God.

A convert to Judaism today is even more rare than a convert to Catholicism was a century ago. It is instinctive in Jews to ask, "Why should this fellow want to join a persecuted race? What is he up to? What does he hope to gain?" If the average Jew had any conception of the gruelling experience a prospective proselyte has to face, and how long he has to face it, before he can even be seriously considered for reception into the fold, I am sure he would change his attitude. The survival of the "Ghetto mentality", whereby the Jew by some atavistic process seems to imagine that if once in a decade, or even once in a century, a Christian joins the ranks of Jewry, the Church will send them all to the stake, is nothing short of amazing in the twentieth century. There are innumerable Jews who could not be more scared for their skins if the Inquisition were still in active existence.

Hundreds of years of persecution have driven the Jew, sad to say, into a violent distaste for any publicity concerning his religion. His instinct is to practise it in the dead of night and behind bolted doors. And in public he will go to any lengths to convince his Christian neighbour that he is not really religious and that a person cannot, after all, help it if he happens to have been born a Jew. This is not true of all the race, of course, but nevertheless the mentality is deplorably widespread.

From all I hear, a striking example of Jewish reluctance to come out into the open is apparent in present-day South Africa. One has to make great allowances, needless to say, for the fact that the Jews there find themselves in a very precarious situation living in a land saddled with a totalitarian régime; but it still remains difficult to suppress a certain feeling of contempt for the attitude of South African Jewry in maintaining such a complete silence on the burning issue of racial discrimination. My sentiments on this matter are greatly influenced, no doubt, by my deep regard for African and Asiatic peoples and my desire to come more and more closely *en rapport* with them. The fact remains, however, that racial discrimination is absolutely in opposition to Jewish principles. South African Jewry, by sitting on the fence, has preserved its own comfort but betrayed its history.

When Hitler was persecuting the Jews our people expected, and rightly so, that the democratic world would cry out in protest at his brutalities. Whether it is that diamonds mean more to South African Jews than the ethics of their forefathers can only be surmised, and it is common knowledge that they are outstandingly generous to charities and of a high commercial integrity. But this timid reticence in face of outrageous racial discrimination is a negation of what Judaism has always stood for. Their Chief Rabbi is said to be a powerful man in dealing with those under his thumb, but it would appear from a distance as though he will not say "Boo!" to a goose outside his own community.

It was Dean Inge who once said that every country gets the Jews it deserves. I feel it possible to go still further and say that the Jew is what the Gentile makes him. Shakespeare's Shylock was the unhappy product of centuries after centuries of cruel persecution. In the last two thousand years millions of Jews have been ruthlessly slaughtered, not for any crime but simply because they *were* Jews. Between the rise and fall of Hitler no less than six million Jews were gassed or otherwise done to death. No age of barbarism has competed with the horrors of our own century. It is a terrible indictment of our so-called progressive age that such diabolical acts could still be perpetrated, and above all in Europe. It should make one feel the more gratitude for such influential friends of the Jews as our times have produced—such men as Dr. Fisher, the Archbishop of Canterbury, Lord Balfour, with his powerful encouragement and help in the early days of Zionism, and even George Bernard Shaw, with his famous pronouncement that "the Jew was born civilized".

If the Jews were a hard, callous, and revengeful people we should have less cause to complain. But I, for my part, have never found them so. True, there were occasions in my experience when they seemed somewhat harsh or lacking in understanding. But let it never be forgotten that a people which has had to fight for its very existence down through the ages develops a thick skin and cannot easily understand the sensitiveness of those who wince at the pin-pricks of life.

It is an unfortunate but undeniable fact that Jews tend to exhibit the worst as well as the best qualities of their lands of origin. To take but a single example, the Russians are a proverbially cruel people, whose actions it is impossible to assess or predict; and accordingly we find the Russian Jew not without that same streak of ruthlessness in his make-up. And it is also most unhappily true that the worst specimens of humanity are generally represented as typifying their race or religion.

Miscarriage of justice in this respect is most liable to occur when a race is distinguished by particular kinds of names or physical characteristics. A Cohen or a Murphy will stand out as an obvious target for minority-baiters, while the mass of delinquent Smiths, Browns, or Robinsons pass unnoticed.

And the popular Press, which should, as part and parcel of its vocation, crusade in the cause of justice, all too frequently goes out of its way to stress racial or religious origins. Every Jew is a Shylock, every Irishman a troublemaker, and every German a potential Nazi.

People who never in their lives have even spoken to a Jew will claim infallibility as authorities on the subject of Jewish ethics, morality, and religious tenets. There have been numerous occasions in European history when thousands of innocent Jews have been burnt alive by fanatical mobs who, without a shred of evidence, embarked on wholesale massacre of harmless men, women, and children just because some malicious Jew-hater started a rumour. Racial discrimination, however, is the putrescent fruit of ignorance and mass hysteria, and thus one is bound to find a certain measure of excuse for the benighted folk of the Dark Ages wherein persecution of Jewry on this wholesale scale took its rise.

There were popes and bishops in those days who protested against those pogroms but, alas, they were in an almost negligible minority. The Jews were blamed for famine, drought, pestilence, and even earthquakes. And in our own lifetime they have been charged with foul deeds which Hitler's own agents had perpetrated. I personally have sat at table with high dignitaries of the Church as well as lay readers when they have given utterance to the most absurd, calumniating sentiments against Jews in general. In most other matters such cultured men would display an amazing degree of tolerance; but the Jew appeared to be a fearsome bogey-man surviving as a legacy of their nursery days, when some anxious nanny had related the story of the death of Jesus with all the trimmings. Some of my learned friends admitted quite frankly that they had known no Jews personally. None of them had ever visited a Jewish family or had any desire to do so. The majority had gained their impressions either through hearsay or through what they had read in their newspapers.

One meets otherwise intelligent people who will find excuses for Hitler, Nero, or the most wilful murderer of modern times, but for a Jew there can be no excuse. Simply to be a Jew is in itself a crime. And the anti-Semite will not even trouble himself to get his facts straight—facts which, were he to do so, would destroy in a moment the entire structure of his prejudices. One of the most sacred tenets of Judaism, for example, is its prohibition of the shedding of human blood. The law regarding blood consumption in meats, is regulated by their having to be salted and soaked in water for 2 hours. And even one blood spot inside an egg, makes the egg unfit or "trefah" for the observant Jew. Yet the "Ritual Murder" charges in which Jews were accused of killing Christian boys to obtain blood for use in lieu of wine at the Passover celebration have persisted even into this twentieth century.

Then there is the very prevalent conception that the Jews' sufferings through the ages have been brought down upon their heads by their own unforgiveable sins.

"The Jews killed Jesus"—that was their great crime, and because of that they may have no respite from the stake, the gas-chamber, or expulsion from their homelands. We destroy Hitler, but in secret we approve his vilest act. It may reasonably be asked, of course, why the Jews should be punished for an action which, according to Christian teaching, was essential to man's salvation. It is a basic tenet of Christian doctrine that Jesus freely chose to offer Himself as a victim to secure the world's redemption—that He was sacrificed, that is to say, as an oblation to appease an angry Father. He was to bear upon His own shoulders the sins of the world, including those of the Jews. There would appear, therefore, to be a contradiction in the attitude of some non-Jews in this respect. While on the one hand Jesus saved His persecutors and obtained forgiveness for them, they are nevertheless condemned to ages of indescribable suffering at the hands of good and evil men alike. If there is any logic in this anomalous outlook I have failed to discover it.

Surely the problem of evil has no solution in this life. Jews believe that God is the rewarder of good and evil, but they give to God the whole of eternity in which to dispense His justice. And in the meantime the Jew blames himself rather than others for his misfortunes. Certain non-Jews have wisely remarked that the best moral barometer of any nation is its attitude towards minorities, and particularly towards the Jews. However wicked the Jews may be, they nevertheless seem always to stand at the graves of their enemies. If history proves anything it certainly proves the truth of this. And the unbroken continuity of the Mother Faith, stretching back as it has for four thousand years to God's revelation of His Laws on Sinai, would appear to set the seal upon it.

There is, of course, only one cure for anti-Semitism, and that is knowledge. When the old-time anti-Jewish propaganda on religious grounds, such as that based upon the killing of Jesus, wore thin there arose the new fable that the Jews owned all the banks and deliberately engineered unemployment. Actually, during the period in European history when industrial conditions were at their worst Jews were in obscurity, and even a cursory investigation will reveal how few Jews rule either in industry or in banking. The number of Jews on the Boards of Directors of national newspapers, too, is negligible. Appreciation of the true facts, however, does show signs of being on the increase. The new Gentile generation, growing up side by side with Jews and meeting them in social life, is steadily becoming less liable to infection with the pernicious disease of anti-Semitism.

The chief offence of the Jew from the more modern-style religious standpoint—whenever, that is to say, the religious fanatics are able to produce any reason at all for their attitude—appears to consist in his unwillingness to accept a creed which genuinely offends his conscience. A modern scholar will investigate, with sincere impartiality, the beliefs of Mormons, Latter Day Saints, or, if you like, Hottentots, but will dismiss as irrelevant any claim that Judaism has for nearly five thousand years contributed generously to the spiritual and moral treasury of the world. Most men will accept the Commandments from the hands of Moses and the Psalms from the lips of David, but will conveniently forget that both of these benefactors were, before and above everything, Jews. The essential Jewish teaching on morality is found in the Bible and other Hebraic sources such as the Talmud. The Bible represents the record of the Jewish way of life, and men of impartial judgment should assess Jewish morals and ethics by what is praised or condemned there.

All too often do we hear it said that the Old Testament teaches exclusively the *fear* of God, and that the New Testament reveals by contrast God's *love*. Anyone who knows the Bible, however, must surely realize that the Psalms are saturated with the love and mercy of a Father who cares. And in the Five Books of Moses, too, constant stress is placed upon the loving kindness and compassion which must be shown to the stranger, while severe punishment is decreed for the oppressor of the widow or the fatherless.

The Jewish law ordains justice to all without reservation. The genuine, traditional Jewish attitude towards justice is well illustrated, in fact, by the little story of the merchant who had a precious stone to sell. While he was saying his evening prayers, a dealer came in with an offer to purchase. The merchant, however, disregarded the interruption and continued with his devotions, whereupon his visitor, mistaking the other's silence for refusal, made a more favourable bid. This happened a second and a third time, and eventually, when the prayers were at last concluded, the offer for the stone had trebled. But the merchant refused the increase in price and signified his acceptance of the original offer. In accordance with Jewish principles, he explained that he had duly heard the first offer and had resolved to accept at that price once his prayers were finished. He would not, he said, take advantage of subsequent increases, which were based upon a misunderstanding on the part of his client.

10

The Covenant of Abraham

"No discipline can be without pain."
HAVELOCK ELLIS

"The elements of perfect piety . . . namely fearing God, walking in His ways, loving him, acting sincerely and keeping all the commandments. . . ."
Preface, *Path of the Upright,* M. LUZZATTO (11)

It was during my second year at Carmel College that the Jewish Ecclesiastical Judges quite abruptly decided, as though by a sudden inspiration from on high, to receive me into the fold of Judaism. After all that long, weary wait I could scarcely believe at first that it had really come to pass. But the Beth Din had evidently seen the light, and apparently seen it with a vengeance, for from then on there was a complete change in their attitude. It seemed that overnight I had become a long-lost brother. I knew then that the rest would be a mere matter of routine.

The first step, and a very formidable one, had to be my circumcision. This operation, sometimes performed upon adults for purely medical reasons, is not of so minor a nature as some would have one believe. It involves being incapacitated for three weeks, and the after-effects are distressing in the extreme. Furthermore, there were in my case, as will be seen later, certain circumstances which involved serious complications.

In view of all the stress and strain I had undergone during the past few years, which had had a cumulative effect upon my constitution and nervous system, and of the additional strain bound to be imposed by the forthcoming operation and subsequent period of convalescence, I now considered it a matter of absolute necessity to take a proper holiday—my first for a very long time. The Levy family, who were very good friends of mine through having two of their sons at Carmel, had invited me to spend three weeks of the long vacation with them at their home on the Rock of Gibraltar. I accepted without hesitation, and as it turned out I was to find there, at long last, true rest of body, mind, and soul.

I fell in love with Gibraltar right away. Its peculiar atmosphere gripped me from the first, and to this day it retains its magic hold upon my affections. Apart from the strong English influence resulting from Gibraltar's function as an outpost of Britain—and the population is 100 per cent firm in its desire to remain with Britain, despite the annoyances suffered from Spain on this account—the general setting is one of Hispano-Moorish charm and leisure.

It would be no exaggeration to say that one of the really happy and glorious periods in the history of Islam was that of the exercise of its influence in Spain. Countless poets and other writers have attempted to do justice to the wonders of Moorish Spain, but unfortunately much of the beauty bequeathed by the Moors was destroyed by a fanatical Church. In Granada and Toledo, and also in Cordova, where I later spent many hours, I saw still in existence even now striking remains of the Moors' magnificent civilization. I felt that students of history, art, and religion could not do better than explore Spain, so outstandingly rich in its heritage of Moorish culture.

As such students will doubtless remember, in 711 of the Common Era Tarik was sent from Africa by Musa across the Straits to the mainland, and there won a decisive battle against the Archbishop of Toledo. Both that city and Cordova were taken, though the latter put up a brave resistance. Tarik, to his credit, spared the Christians on payment of tribute; and he showed even greater mercy to the Jews, who, more than grateful to escape from the tyranny of an intolerant Church, had given him material help.

The Moors, although they did not extend their conquest any farther to the North, nevertheless retained a firm hold of the mainland until at last they were driven out in the fifteenth century. Following their expulsion, the Muhammedan faith became restricted to a few specific areas. Despite its influence in Asia, it has never come to rank as a world religion, notwithstanding that it is estimated to number approximately 230,000,000 adherents—a goodly array for any faith. It was reserved to Christianity to provide the Gentiles with a religion in one form or another.

Islam I have always considered a very practical religion. For although it has room among its conceptions for saints, miracles, and other supernatural manifestations, it does not press all its followers into the avowed acceptance of multivarious dogmas. A man is required to believe in One God, Allah, and in Muhammed as His supreme prophet. He must recite prayers at prescribed hours of the day, he must abstain from alcohol and certain forbidden foods. But Islam contains none of the rationalized mysteries so prominent in Christian doctrine. I have always felt that when the Moors were expelled from Spain that country was much the poorer for their going. Large numbers of Spaniards welcomed the simplicity of the Muslim faith and had been glad to be rid of the ever-increasing image-worship as practised by the Church of those days.

As I have remarked elsewhere, the waning influence of Islam has been a matter of regret to me, and that regret came back with renewed force as I surveyed the relics of its heyday in Spain. But these sad reflections did not last long, for all around me were the fascinating sights and sounds of Gibraltar to provide distraction. The quaint, narrow streets with their Spanish-style equipages and mule-drawn carts rumbling over the cobbles, and the gaily decorated bazaars and colourful shops and cafés, offered such a welcome change from the modern world's drab uniformity. And on my daily climb up the Rock I was able to gaze across the blue bay, with the coast of Spain supplying as romantic a background as could be imagined, and Africa rising majestically in the distance.

The Jewish community in this fascinating colony has a wonderful tradition; in fact, it is often called the "Little Jerusalem", and I would not hesitate to say it is unique west of Palestine. Its rabbis have included saints and scholars known the world over, such as, for example, the late Moses Benaim, the revered parent of the Jewish community's life president. The Mayor of Gibraltar, moreover, the Hon. Joshua Hassan, M.V.O., is a practising Jew. Here I was to experience something which is not to be found in any other place outside of Israel, and which helped me materially to see Judaism in its old, traditional setting: namely, the closing of every Jewish place of business on the Sabbath. No matter how worldly a Gibraltar Jew may be, he will close down his shop both on the Sabbath and on Festival Days. Whenever a big passenger ship, particularly an American one, docks on the Sabbath, the Jewish shopkeepers lose thousands of pounds' worth of business. For anyone to be able to display this indifference to money matters he must possess a deeply rooted faith. And that is precisely what these delightful people do possess.

The colony, with its four religions and three languages, is a veritable League of Nations; for Catholics, Jews, Indians, and a wide variety of other races and creeds dwell together there in unbroken harmony, thanks to a spirit of tolerance all too rare. Before the War there had been a thousand Jews on the Rock, but many had not returned from evacuation, and now the number was reduced to a mere six hundred. Yet there were no fewer than six synagogues to cater for the spiritual needs of this faithful remnant, the services at all of them being conducted according to the *Sephardic* custom.

As readers may or may not know, *Sephardim* is the term applied to the Spanish and Portuguese Jews, many of whom, when expelled from their homelands in the days of the Inquisition, settled in Amsterdam and also in London. They were at first compelled to remain in hiding, but with the emancipation of Jews and Catholics in the mid-nineteenth century they emerged into the light of day. The *Sephardim* employ the same modern pronunciation of Hebrew that is current in Israel, as opposed to the *Ashkenazi* pronunciation used by Jews coming from Germany, Poland, and Eastern countries.

The *Sephardim* have their own synagogues, and their cathedral synagogue for England is Bevis Marks, in the City of London. They also have their own leader, called the *Haham*, or "Learned One", the kindly and greatly beloved Dr. Solomon Gaon. But though they employ their own liturgy and have this separate leader as distinct from Dr. Brodie, the Chief Rabbi of Great Britain, they are on excellent terms with the *Ashkenazi* community and likely to remain so.

For many years the *Sephardim* considered themselves the aristocrats of Jewry, and would not even marry *Ashkenazi* Jews. Happily, however, this nonsense has become a thing of the past. Some very distinguished *Sephardim* have in recent times graced English public life, Lord Belisha, the Montefiore, and the Sassoon families providing specially noteworthy examples.

The unique *Sephardic* chants which I heard in the synagogues of Gibraltar struck me as being far more Hebraic in flavour than those heard in Eastern Europe, as indeed they are. In fact, my first impression was that Gibraltar's Judaism was perhaps the soundest and most deeply rooted I had as yet encountered anywhere. However, there were signs, alas, that the faith was beginning to weaken. The Jewish youths cared less about Judaism than had their fathers. Unlike the Catholic young people, they had no youth movement and no youth leaders. The sad result was that they had suffered morally and took advantage of the temptations offered by loose-living girls across the Spanish frontier. All religions on the Rock were in a commendably healthy state, and everything seemed to be well under control with the single exception of this unhappy feature of immorality on the part of Jewish adolescents. At the Jewish Club for adults I gave a lecture on youth problems, but the interest which it aroused, though considerable for the time being, was lamentably short-lived.

The dominant faith in Gibraltar, as in Malta, is Roman Catholicism, and the local Catholics are much more zealous than are their co-religionists in neighbouring Spain. They were trained, it seems, in the strict school of what we may term English Romanism by Bishop Fitzgerald, a truly devoted pastor who had, by the end of his saintly and fruitful life, both given new impetus to the Roman Church in Gibraltar and dominated all higher education in the colony. Roman Catholics in England, especially those who have not travelled, are apt to imagine that their co-religionists in Spain and Italy are as devout as they are themselves. This, however, is a major fallacy. The majority of Catholics on the Continent appear to think nothing of regularly missing Mass and thus risking the consequences of frequent mortal sin. And in moral life, too, there would appear to be some inconsistency, as the following incident will demonstrate.

One day, with the idea of using up my visas, I decided to take a walk across the frontier into Spain. On reaching the little town of La Linea I started looking round the market-place. I had been thus engaged for only a few minutes when I was accosted by a very respectable-looking man who courteously inquired whether I wished to be shown the local places of interest and offered his services as guide. I accepted the offer, and it was some time before I began to suspect the underlying purpose of the man's solicitude. Eventually, however, he began to ask me personal questions such as could not fail to start me wondering: was I married or single? Was I of military or civilian status? And so on.

In an attempt to head him off from possibly still more intimate questioning, I asked to be shown the ancient church. Unperturbed, he escorted me into the sacred building, switched on the lights at the side-altars, crossed himself very elaborately, genuflected before the Sacred Sacrament, and generally conducted himself as a worthy son of the Holy Mother Church. He pointed out the various features of the edifices, explaining their significance in detail, little suspecting how much I, an ordained priest, could have taught him. When we at last emerged from the church, my guide came promptly to the point.

"Would the senor care to visit a house where they have specially Spanish girls?" he inquired in his exquisitely courteous manner.

Fearing that I might turn upon the man with righteous wrath, I made the excuse that there were friends waiting for me at the frontier. I pushed a ten-peseta note into his ready hand, bade him a hasty farewell, and hurried back to the Rock, determined never again to leave it unaccompanied.

In all my experience as a priest in Britain it had never occurred to me that such a mentality as that exhibited by this La Linea guide could go hand in hand with Catholic civilization. Although it is not for any man to throw stones at his neighbour, it had, of course, been impossible for me to remain unaware that Catholics were inclined on occasion to tell lies, to get drunk, and even to resort to thieving. And there was also the fairly frequent occurrence of sexual promiscuity. But I had associated these sins or weaknesses with the social background of the long-oppressed working-class immigrants from Ireland. However, I had heard stories enough of the immorality to be found in Catholic countries, and that Catholics living in those countries seemed to be satisfied with a nominal faith, bothering little about religion outside of baptism, marriage, and burial. And often, by contrast, I had heard it said that native English Roman Catholics, attending Mass regularly and leading self-disciplined lives, were the best to be found in the world. What staggered me in the episode just related was the dual aspect of religious life in Catholics as represented by my sanctimonious guide on that occasion. I sincerely felt that it stemmed from an undue reliance upon the sacramental system, whereby so much personal responsibility to God was absolved or transferred to priests, saints, or the Virgin.

Towards the end of my visit I received a telegram from

the doctor in charge of arrangements for my circumcision, saying that he had fixed an appointment for me in the following week. Although my whole recent life had been leading up to this event, it was with the utmost regret that I bade farewell to Gibraltar and to my wonderful friends, the Levy family. I considered them typical of the local Hebrew community, gracious, hospitable, and high-principled. A son of theirs, Abraham Levy, was one of my own pupils, and is at present dedicating himself to Rabbinic studies under Dr. Epstein at Jews' College, in London. This college is established for the training of rabbis and teachers, and now has become a residential seminary.

Altogether, there were quite a number of pupils from the colony at Carmel, and I had observed that they all shared that high grade of character which seemed to spring from this inspired community. As for Gibraltar itself, it had truly been an oasis in my vast and weary spiritual desert, a veritable haven of moral rehabilitation.

Armed with the good wishes of my friends, I set off to face my ordeal. Arriving back in England on a Friday, I went to spend the week-end before my operation at the Hendon home of Mrs. Philip Cohen. Providence seems usually to supply trustworthy guides for those who seek Its will, and it was in her home that I learned the ways of a Jewish house.

Mrs. Cohen had lost her husband, a very distinguished official in the Air Ministry, five years before. It was to my close friend and spiritual guide, the Reverend Leslie Hardman, the minister of the beautiful Hendon synagogue, to whom I was indebted for the introduction to this good daughter of Israel. With this introduction he had performed a *mitzvah* * of inestimable value, and this was but one of his innumerable kindnesses. Mr. Hardman became for me the symbol of the ideal minister, deep of sympathy and broad of outlook. I will always remember his goodness to me during

* Good deed.

those critical moments. It was the Hendon Synagogue that I first visited. The services there were beautifully conducted, and the building itself lends great dignity to the proceedings. There I gradually found a spiritual home.

On the Sunday following my return to England I entered the nursing home where the operation was to be performed. The moment I went into that operating-theatre I suddenly realized that I was standing absolutely alone in the world. It would have been impossible, in fact, to think of a more isolated situation. To begin with, the nursing home was non-Jewish, and I could see at once that everybody there was puzzled by my having come there for such a purpose. I should, of course, have insisted upon the operation taking place at the London Jewish Hospital. As it was, the environment added immeasurably to my distress and sense of desolation.

When being placed on the operating-table, however, I reminded myself that despite the darkness which enwrapped my spirit, God was very near to me at that moment, and I composed myself to offer the sacrifice as an act of union with the Creator who had called upon me to sign and seal in the Covenant of Blood my renunciation of all false faith and doctrine, in the spirit of our ancestor, Abraham.

The anaesthetist, for some reason, found it extremely difficult to send me off to sleep. After several efforts, however, I did at last lose consciousness, but not before I had called out, in the loudest voice I could muster, the traditional invocation for that fateful moment: "*Shema Yisrael, Adonai Elohanu Adonai Echad!*" which translated means "Hear O Israel! The Lord our God, the Lord is One!" No doubt the hospital staff were considerably startled.

Kind friends sent messages, cables came in from my friends in Gibraltar. Mr. Hardman visited me and offered to supply Kosher food or anything else that might be required. Colleagues at Carmel came to see me too, and my *mohel*,* Dr.

* The surgeon who performs the circumcision.

Bernard Homa, was the essence of patience and humanity. In brief, I was no longer alone and isolated.

Since no Jewish funds exist for the assistance of proselytes and I had no desire to run up heavy bills at the nursing home on my own account I returned to Carmel College earlier than I would have done otherwise. I was given a very pleasant room in the new school premises at Mongewell Park, and there I proceeded to relax so far as possible in preparation for the coming school term. Thanks to my restless nature, however, I wanted to become active too soon, and one night, as might have been expected, the wound of my operation received a severe knock. It bled profusely, and naturally I was very alarmed. Two of the younger masters promptly sent for the school doctor. Had he been available all would have been well, for he was a most kindly, understanding soul. But as luck would have it he was absent, and the doctor who came in his place was anything but agreeable.

Throwing open the door of my room without ceremony, he barked out, before he had even had the opportunity of examining the trouble, "I hope this is an essential call! If it isn't I shall be really angry!" It was only 10 p.m., but after one glance at the wound he exploded a second time. "Absolutely disgraceful to send for me, and entirely unnecessary!" he snapped, though there before his eyes on the light fawn carpet lay the yards of bandages, soaked in blood. When the doctor, surely a disgrace to his profession, had stamped out of the room, I broke down. In my overwrought condition I saw this cruel incident as Act Two in a drama of martyrdom. God had asked much of me, I told myself, and I had given with all my heart; I could give no more. . . .

After a few weeks the stitches were taken out, and this again caused me the most acute pain. Dr. Rosen himself drove me home, I remember, and under the balm of his sympathy I appreciated anew that warm humanity which lay deep within his fiery nature. Then followed the ritual of submersion and recitation of the Act of Faith. As did Jesus when subjected to the same ceremony by John the Baptist, I descended a flight of steps into a special bath, called the *mikvah*, and there dipped completely under water three times. This, I should explain, is not a sacrament, but simply a ritual cleansing. As one descends, one purifies the heart and soul with will and mind and with the help of God. Never before in my life had I felt so uplifted. The suffering and well-nigh total eclipse of human joy and consolation had given place to a profound assurance and an inward peace which, unlike my former faith, the most violent of circumstances would not manage to disturb. My whole being, my heart, my mind, my soul—all were centred upon my Creator. There was no division of my loyalty, and I knew with an overwhelming certainty that God gave back all in return.

I felt that now my spirit had finally found peace in Judaism. People, of course, still mattered greatly, but they could not destroy my union with God. For inherent in my new-found faith was the factor which above all had drawn me to it—direct reliance solely upon Him, not upon intermediaries. I felt that I had won through to something so dazzlingly sublime as to render insignificant the obstacles I had been called upon to surmount. And truly there is no other religion which places so many obstacles in the way of converts as does Judaism.

My experience in this respect, in fact, had driven me to a firm conclusion that only the very sincere, or else the very insane, would submit to the tests and trials imposed by the Beth Din. I fully understood and concurred that a candidate should be thoroughly tested, but I could not help feeling that the management of affairs, once the trial was over, left much to be desired.

The arrangements for my circumcision, for example, had been vague and obscure, so that I myself had been left to carry through all the necessary negotiations, with the resultant misapprehensions. Although it was obviously fitting that such an operation should take place in a Jewish institution, it had actually been performed in a nursing home where I was surrounded by puzzled non-Jews whose detached attitude made me feel like a displaced person. I was, and still am, strongly of the opinion that the authorities should display a more sympathetic and helpful interest in the arrangements for the reception of converts, and that the whole procedure, in fact, should be efficiently re-organized by the Beth Din.

In cases where circumcision is required a Jewish hospital, and no other ought, to carry out this greatly underestimated operation. Many uninformed people are under the impression that such an operation is merely a forty-eight hours' affair, but that idea is far from the truth. It requires three full weeks before the patient is restored to normality, and even then he must be careful. I realize, of course, that the Beth Din has many problems to face, but the efficient handling of these cases is of vital importance. The proselyte has already suffered in a variety of ways, and his further sufferings under this operation should certainly not be unduly increased by the unsympathetic environment of a non-Jewish institution.

If I have rather heavily underlined this point, even at the cost of repetition, it is not from any desire to ventilate personal feelings, but solely in the fervent hope that others may find their path more pleasant at this critical juncture. And there is also the financial angle. Although fortunately I was in a position to find money for the heavy expenses involved, I should not like to think that an impecunious person would find himself unable to become a Jew on that account. It seems very strange that a proselyte should be called upon to pay all the costs of hospital treatment, more especially in cases where he may already be in difficulties. The National Health Scheme does not recognize the operation, and in consequence there is no assistance to be had from the State either. If the operation were to be performed in a Jewish hospital, as is so obviously appropriate, the expense could then be kept to a minimum, and the patient could also have Kosher food as well as enjoy a Jewish atmosphere in general.

But the defects in the handling of converts are by no means confined to this circumcision period. The proselyte must still be prepared to pass through a long spell of loneliness. His new brethren will not feel towards him as he feels towards them. He has left all behind because he loves the House of Israel, but he cannot expect the Jewish community either to appreciate that or even believe it. A friend of mine once told me in those early days. "You will have to convince them one by one." And so it proved to be for some considerable time, though today I am able to count a good number of convinced friends and rejoice in the happiness of their company and comradeship.

However, one is bound in all fairness to try to see the other side of the picture, and one must never lose sight of the fact that Judaism is in no sense a "missionary" religion. Indeed, unless one is strongly inspired to do so, one may never discover it at all; for the Jewish authorities themselves deliberately keep their treasures in heavily barred cellars as a matter of policy. In my own case, for example, there were people in authority who suggested, even after I had taken the final step, that I might have done more good by staying where I was. They were evidently thinking of my potential value as a philo-Semitic clergyman rather than of my conscience and self-respect.

I am not writing this in a spirit of reproach, but simply because I feel the facts should be realized and understood. The problem as viewed from the authorities' point of view may be summed up thus: "Do we really desire proselytes? And when they come, what are we to do about them?" To find an effective answer to these questions must eventually demand serious attention on the part of the authorities. Are we to assume that an Abraham or a Ruth are to be expected only at infrequent intervals, or will an increasing flow of converts follow as a result of a wider understanding of

Judaism? Reason would surely indicate that there will be just such a growing influx. Could we cope with such a situation, or do we have an inferiority complex about Judaism, that it is not good enough to attract the average Gentile?

The attitude of Judaism towards converts is, I believe, quite unique among all the world's religions. Most religions are "missionary" religions, but Judaism is not. And the seeming indifference does not arise from lack of charity on the part of the religion itself, although the attitude of individual Jews towards proselytes is often without excuse and, indeed, altogether beyond comprehension. The simple, basic fact is this: Judaism teaches that the righteous of all religions inherit the life to come. There are certain other religions—the "totalitarian" religions is my name for them—which consider membership of their own particular faith essential to salvation, but Judaism harbours no such narrow concept. That is why there has been so little persecution by Jews and so much of it on the part of her two daughter religions, Christianity and Islam. The Jew is prepared to live and let live and cherishes no urge to press others into his form of belief, deeming it unnecessary in view of his tenet that the prospect of salvation is already shared by all.

From this assumption that the worthy of every faith shall inherit life eternal, a fundamental principle of Judaism, follows naturally and logically the moral attitude of the Jew towards the non-Jew. There is no falsehood more disgusting than that which maintains that Jews have one standard of justice for their own creed and another less-rigid set of laws to be observed towards the Gentile. The Jew is bound by his religion to hold that an unjustice committed against a non-Jew is even more grievous than one committed against a co-religionist. Indeed, my own experience has been that Jews are kinder to strangers than to their own brethren. Non-Jewish employees are extremely privileged as a rule in any Jewish organization, if not actually given preferential treatment. Neither does any Jew worthy of the name hold the honour of a Gentile woman in less respect than that of a Jewess. Isolated instances of immoral Jews have, as in so many other matters, given rise to an entirely false notion.

Gentiles frequently experience difficulty in finding maids because there is such a rush, even on the part of practising Catholic girls, to secure posts in Jewish homes. These girls are strongly encouraged by their employers to attend Mass and otherwise follow out their religious training. Salaries and holidays are far more generous than in the majority of Christian households; the maid finds, in fact, a home away from home in the Jewish household, but with the difference that it is often a kinder home. And great vigilance, it should be added, is exercised regarding their moral welfare.

The first experience of Jewish morality that came my way had been in my dealings with the London Beth Din. Never in my life have I felt the impact of sincerity and unswerving justice so strongly as I did there. The *Dayonim*, the Ecclesiastical Judges, were living models of uprightness. True, they exasperated me at times by their absent-mindedness or apparent lack of courtesy, but I was never for a single moment in any doubt as to their sincerity. Always there was that complete freedom from compromise and humbug which blew like a refreshing breeze through a world putrescent with deceit and duplicity.

To return, however, after this digression, to the subject of Judaism's refusal to seek converts even to the point of hiding her light under a bushel. I maintain that Jews have undoubtedly gone too far in this attitude of reticence, the reason for which is so largely a historical one. Constant persecution through the centuries has unquestionably bred an inferiority complex—so much so, in fact, that non-Jews are left with the impression that Judaism has no message to give to the world. This is quite untrue. It is one thing not to be a missionary religion, and quite another not to have a mission.

But many Jews seem to be entirely unaware that a Jewish world-mission exists. The general attitude seems to be that of being extremely lucky to be permitted to live, and that even if Christianity is not the real solution, Judaism at least has no alternative to offer. Whenever I have spoken to Jews about the contribution Judaism has made in the past to religion and morals, they stare at me as though I were relating a fairy-tale.

This ignorance of the Jewish heritage is unfortunately a phenomena among all people of the world, irrespective of their religion. Jews should certainly spare no effort to make each new generation fully conscious of the inestimable treasures of culture, morals, and religion which their forefathers have bequeathed to the world in general and not to Jews alone. And yet even among Jewish Youth there is a great deal of ignorance of their past. The contemporary Jew seems more anxious for the opinion of the Gentile world than for his own pride and self-respect. He will let down the interests of Jewry and their own brethren rather than offend a non-Jew, though this fawning upon the necks of Gentiles brings upon him from the latter the contempt he so richly deserves.

And what, precisely, is Judaism's mission, it may be asked. My answer is that the Jewish religion exists to bear witness before the entire world that there is One God Only, who alone must be adored and worshipped with all our being. Jews believe that in God's own good time error will vanish from the hearts and minds of men, and that the Truth as revealed to Moses will then prevail. They give the Almighty His own time in which to cover the earth with the knowledge of Him as the waters cover the sea. We do not grab souls from the imaginary fires of hell nor consign to eternal perdition those who differ from us in belief. The Jewish faith is eminently rational, entirely free from the anxiety-neuroses so common to missionary faiths. Certainly we care, but we also remember that God cares. Unlike the fussy little man who touched the ark to keep it straight, we bear in mind that God has many ways of bringing His children home. We are not consumed with religious prejudice, nor do we seek to challenge others on the validity of their beliefs. Let their conscience be their guide! is our slogan.

11

My Spirit finds Peace

"My crown is called content."
SHAKESPEARE

"The Gaon of Wilna is reported to have said, he would not like an angel as teacher, who would reveal to him all the mysteries of the Scriptures. This befits the world to come, in *this* world only things which are acquired by hard labour and great struggle are of any value."
SOLOMON SCHECHTER, *Studies in Judaism.* (12c)

AT Carmel the active round of communal life, the teaching, housemastering, marking of exercises and all the other items which made up our daily routine, gave place on Friday evenings to a peace and spiritual rest that was past all description. As Sabbath descended upon the school, the presence of God seemed very close. Rows and rows of boys, smiling of face and clad in their best, sang those ancient Hebrew melodies which have fortified and consoled so many generations of their ancestors, for untold centuries. The workaday weekday world seemed a million miles away. There shone on every face a sweet enchantment. The lighted candles, the fresh young voices of the boys, and the imposing presence of Dr. Rosen, reminiscent of some prophet of old, transported any visitors to a spiritual world beyond all expression of appreciation. They could only sit breathless, absorbing the spiritual influence of this so singular little world. The Lord God of Israel stood beside them. And then after supper it was from time to time Dr. Rosen's custom to invite the staff to visit him in his house. And there the gathering would engage in stimulating conversation until the hour came to wish one another *Shabbat Shalom*—"A Peaceful Sabbath"—and retire to one's own quarters.

The serene contentment of those Eve of Sabbath observances at Carmel invariably led me to reflect how very shortsighted was the growing modern tendency to neglect this heaven-sent respite. Most of us are agreed, I believe, that the world today is suffering more from mental than from physical illness. The vast and ever-growing army of psychiatrists, whose services are in such constant demand by a large section of the community, provides a clear indication that all is not well with modern man.

This unhappy state of affairs unquestionably arises in large measure from an almost universal neglect of one of our Creator's fundamental laws. It was no arbitrary act of Providence which decreed that man must abstain from labour on the seventh day of each week. On the contrary, that Commandment is founded upon man's very nature, as designed and implanted in him by God.

Man is able to work for six days of the week, but he requires, as a *sine qua non* for his mental, moral, and spiritual health, one complete day away from mundane pursuits. He is thereby renewed and uplifted both as a human being and as a child of God. This break with the workaday world ensures his release from slavery. Money, machines, and all the other adjuncts of Mammon are put in their proper place as he rises for that brief interval above their grip and tyranny.

The myopic type of Jew, failing to appreciate this blessing, regards the Sabbath as a purely negative and annoying prohibition coming to prevent him from doing all the profitable, enjoyable things he wants to do. He misses the whole point. He cannot see that the Commandment is not a burden but a godsend; it is a healing medicine and a revitalizing tonic.

The Jew who desires to rush about by bus or car on the Sabbath; the Jew who needs must hang on to the telephone throughout the Sabbath; the Jew who cannot wait until the morrow to open his business correspondence—this Jew is rejecting freedom. He insists on being a slave. He acclaims the world his master for seven days a week, so that neither his mind nor his body and soul can truthfully be called his own. This man's spiritual, intellectual, and physical life all remain at low ebb while the poor wretch grovels on the plane of materialism. He is, in fact, but half a man and less than half a Jew.

The Jew, even if he does not go to synagogue, can at least observe the Sabbath. It is, of course, much more desirable that he should pray in company with his brethren and follow with them the reading of the Sacred Law of Moses, but Judaism has never depended upon synagogue attendance. It is the home that is the altar of Judaism, and in the Jewish home every vital act of religion can and does take place.

Again, when Jews do go to synagogue they all too often seem to treat the place with an unseemly lack of reverence. They tend to exchange gossip in between the more vital parts of the service and make themselves too much at home in general. The United Synagogue in England is endeavouring to introduce a greater dignity and decorum into its places of worship; but since every Jew is a law unto himself, this will take time and much patience. It is a case of "hasten slowly" for those who seek to discipline Jewry in any department of its activities.

No man of tender susceptibilities would be well advised to embark upon the stormy seas of the Jewish ministry! It is a regular practice for the members of the congregation during the sermon, which is rarely of too high a quality, to tear the preacher to shreds with all manner of comments upon his faults and failings. Even the late Chief Rabbi, Dr. Hertz, who was about as tough as one could reasonably expect any clergyman to be, was only just tough enough. The present Chief Rabbi, for his part, is a diplomat and strives to keep on the right side of all and sundry, though that is sometimes a high price to pay for peace. But perhaps he finds it the only possible course. Certainly he is the soul of kindness, and I have never met a man of greater charm.

Many of our Jewish preachers, I have noticed, seem to have nothing to say, though it must be admitted they say it well. Others, on the other hand, and they are in the minority, have plenty to say, but say it so poorly that few can derive benefit from their wisdom and knowledge. The training of Jewish ministers is a problem which calls for very careful thought. We are still very much in the experimental stage. Great though my sympathy is with the Rabbinate and

Jewish ministry, the fact has to be faced that in the past these have constituted one of the really weak links in the Communal chain.

It is clear that some men who embark upon the sacred work have absolutely no vocation for it. As professional or business men they might well have been highly successful, but in this vital sphere they are misfits. I have long felt it a sad thing that the Community should respect its ministers so little, but sadder still that the latter should give so little reason for respect. Some among our spiritual leaders have no spirituality, nor even dignity. By their conspicuous lack of personal qualities and of devotion to duty they make themselves natural targets for uncharitable attacks by their congregants. Much of a minister's difficulty arises from the fact that he is at the mercy of these last-named, who can and often do pursue him to the very doors. Knowing how very unkind and even spiteful people are capable of being towards one another, it is an easy matter to feel sympathy with the laymen's reverend employee.

Until a more satisfactory state of affairs comes into being, the minister's only protection, apart from a very thick skin, must lie in a genuine superiority in both the secular and the Rabbinic realms. If the minister be inferior in learning, general culture, or Rabbinics he is fighting a hopeless battle. The Christian priest is respected just because he is a priest. The Jewish minister is despised just because he is a minister, and only on the strength of his endowments can he reverse that unworthy situation. We pay our prophets the compliment of stoning them, but our lesser lights we condemn to the more lingering death of contempt. The attitude of some Jewish parents in this connection is nothing short of disgraceful. They give the impression that they would rather have their sons sweep the streets than devote their lives to the most urgently needed work to which a man can turn his hand in this world.

It is clear that the remedy lies in the training of our future ministers. A residential college has been a *sine qua non* for the successful production of dedicated Rabbis and ministers, and it is a tremendous step forward that Jews' College in London, which supplies our spiritual and moral leaders, and is therefore the most vital of our institutions in England, has now become a residential one. For a day college, however excellent, is no substitute for a *yeshiva*, or seminary. The student must imbibe over a period of years that continuous atmosphere which will form the background to his future active and often very secular life. But with this changed status of Jews' College we are not lacking, thank God, in a small but zealous band of youths who, if well trained and properly supported, will turn the tide of religious apathy in Anglo-Jewry. Many years ago, when as a priest I visited Jews' College to inspect its library, I was told by a responsible official that the Jewish community, when it got good ministers, should treat them properly, and how right he was. And now our Ecclesiastical Authorities are endeavouring to ensure that the products of our colleges are sent out so equipped that they may have no need to assert themselves in order to gain respect, but will rather command it by virtue of an unchallenged superiority in culture, both Hebraic and secular.

It might be a very wise move, I consider, to send the best students from Jews' College to Oxford or Cambridge. Both they and their future congregants would benefit immeasurably from this additional polish. It is my feeling that if a youth has a strong sense of vocation for the ministry he should proceed to Rabbinical studies after gaining his General Certificate and then, with the foundation of a sound Jewish knowledge, go on to university. For the majority, affiliation to London University would appear to suffice. There should always, however, be a few ministers who are graduates of the older, residential universities. And while on this subject I would suggest that resident chaplains could with advantage have been appointed at Oxford and Cambridge to safeguard the interests of all Jewish undergraduates. Such chaplains should need to be men of strong religious convictions, together with a deep and wide culture. The benefit which non-Jewish undergraduates derive from their Christian chaplains makes it difficult to understand why such an obvious need as that for Jewish "opposite numbers" has not long ago been met.

In talking of the institution called a *yeshivoth*, it is well to remember that is the name given to the Houses of Hebraic Learning where, in the days when Jewish life was lived in strongly Hebraic surroundings, men and boys in every walk of life studied the Sacred Law and the commentaries of the great Rabbis, the Talmud with its interpretation of Maimonides and Rashi. Not only those destined to become Rabbis, but all and sundry, from future tradesmen to future statesmen, would consider this study an essential part of their training for life. Many businessmen were great Hebraic scholars, and there were Rabbis who carried on a trade or profession to support their learning.

Unhappily this tradition has weakened considerably in the past fifty years, especially during the interval between the two world wars. There are signs of a revival, it is true, but the conditions of modern life, with its hectic pace, render a life of study very difficult, particularly for those engaged in the rush of commercial or even professional activities.

As for other media of religious instruction, the part-time evening classes so popular in the old days have been superseded by classes conducted by the Religious Boards. However, the great Jewish Day School movement, especially as promoted by the Schoenfeld Schools in London, has undoubtedly reclaimed many sections of Anglo-Jewry which would otherwise have been lost for ever.

A badly felt need in the past has been that of Jewish boarding schools. There have been several attempts to establish such institutions; but with one or two exceptions these proved abortive. The reason for this protracted apathy towards boarding schools is not hard to discover. It arises from the predominant feature of Jewish education: namely, that it centres upon instruction in the home and holds that for the Jewish home there is no substitute. But when parents are themselves ignorant of their heritage, how can they pass it on to their children?

Passing on to consider the education and welfare of those young people who have left school, I feel compelled, speaking as one who has founded youth movements in non-Jewish circles, to express acute disappointment with the half-hearted and woefully ineffective efforts of Anglo-Jewry. Clubs there are in abundance, it is true, but they cater in the main for those who need no club, thus providing a striking instance of the tendency of our Jewish social reformers to spend far too much time and energy preaching to those who don't need them.

I shall not be exaggerating if I state that 70 per cent of Jewish youth are unattached to any form of Jewish club, society, or synagogue. They are, in fact, merely Jews by birth, and mixed marriages will ensure their children being deprived even of that slight qualification. Some authorities, if suggestions are put forward to them, will answer that these young people are not really Jews, or that even if they are Jews they are not interested. Such an attitude, I submit, should disqualify anyone from leadership in the Community. If, in place of indulging in petty squabbles, our efforts for youth could be amalgamated, and thus placed on a really effective basis, the leakage from Jewry could undoubtedly be stemmed.

There are, for example, thousands of young Jews working in the City of London and in the West End. If these young people wish to eat Kosher food they must either pay exorbitant prices or content themselves with sandwiches. A series of Kosher canteens could do much to save our young workers from drifting into forbidden paths. If any army marches on its stomach, it is certainly the Jewish working community. Maybe I am crying for the moon, but I am convinced that what is really needed in central London is a Jewish equivalent of, say, the Y.M.C.A. establishment in Tottenham Court Road, which is, as a matter of fact, patronized by quite a large number of young Jews, both native Londoners and hailing from the provinces. The situation is just another instance of those who possess the vision lacking the means, and *vice versa.*

If my observations seem somewhat critical, at least they proceed from a heart which desires good for all Jewry rather than merely for a favoured section that stands in no need of social or spiritual saviours. And in all fairness I cannot leave this subject without mentioning the really magnificent work being done for students residing in London by the directorate of Hillel House, Euston. Here university students are able to obtain Kosher meals cheaply, and there is living accommodation for a limited number from the provinces. Untold good will result if only this movement can spread to the other universities.

Taking into consideration the various disadvantages encountered by Jewish youth, I feel it is greatly to their credit that they keep as straight a path as they do. The findings of several committees of inquiry have indicated that juvenile delinquency is more rare among Jewish than among non-Jewish young people. That has certainly been my own experience after very close contact with both categories, and I am sure it is largely accounted for by the strength of Jewish family ties. The average Jewish child knows beyond any shadow of doubt that he is wanted and deeply loved by his parents, grandparents, and other relatives, all of whom lavish upon him unceasing affection and attention. A cruel Jewish parent, or a drunken Jewish husband, are things almost unknown. Gentiles, so far as my experience goes, are mostly far inferior to Jews in their standards of parenthood. As a priest, it frequently became one of my most unpleasant duties to rebuke parents for neglecting their children, and even for downright cruelty. But I have never yet seen a neglectful Jewish mother or an unkind Jewish father. They probably do exist here and there, but if so they are few and far between.

In spite of these excellent domestic traits, however, it has to be regretfully admitted that in recent years, as a result of assimilation, our people have begun to copy some of the more reprehensible characteristics of the nations in whose midst they live, as did our ancestors following their departure from Egypt. For there has been an undeniable falling off in the moral conduct of our community. Broken homes are today more frequent than in the days of the Ghetto, and in modern families dubious practices, such as, for example, contraception—though its adherents are able to produce a plausible case in its defence—have crept in to our grave loss. Assuredly we should exercise a firm though sympathetic vigilance over the moral tendencies of our youth, seeing that in their case the temptations of modern life could well endanger the whole future of our people.

The Jew is by nature clean in mind and body. Family life, with its numerous safeguards, its laws of cleanliness and hygiene, has been the bulwark of our race. But nowadays too little moral guidance is being given to our Jewish youth, and the majority of our social and religious leaders seem to be afraid to speak out plainly against evil practices. Let us realize before it is too late that unless we adhere faithfully to our Law, we shall suffer the fate of ancient Greece and Rome, whose decline and fall steadily kept pace with their progressive degradation in moral conduct. The Jewish laws concerning purity both before and after marriage are worthy of close study, and could with profit be copied by the nations. Our chief concern, however, is that our own brethren should remember those sacred laws, inasmuch as in their obedience to them resides the guarantee of our survival as a race and as a chosen instrument of God's purpose for the world.

The ultimate remedy for all our ills, let me repeat, is a general return to the sturdy, well-informed Jewish family life of the past, which was the great strength of our race throughout the ages. Jewish parents are without equal anywhere, and it is to them above all others that we must turn for our hope in the future. The artificial life which has transferred the focus of our existence from the Jewish home to the luxury hotel is a positive menace to our prospects as a people. The Friday night observances, together with all the other traditional institutions of our Jewish way of life, have only to be revived in order to bring about a mighty upsurge of our influence and purpose as a chosen people. The world cannot be offered a more precious treasure than the way of life of the Jewish people, those immortal traditions which flow from Sinai and will continue to flow until the true Messiah shall bring us peace and justice.

It was while staying with Mrs. Philip Cohen that I had become acquainted with the ways of a Jewish home, and the more I saw of them, the more I appreciated their benign influence. The joys of Sabbath, as an example, are chiefly connected with the Jewish home, and on that day an entirely new atmosphere pervades the dwelling. Unlike the synagogue, which is but a focal point, the home represents the very foundation of Judaism, especially on that particular day, the day of rest.

The Christian Sabbath, by contrast, is a more formal and even half social affair. It has never, in fact, really fulfilled the purpose of Sabbath as intended by the Creator. Early in the history of the Church the day itself was changed from the seventh day of the week to the first. The change was entirely unwarranted, and Jesus Himself did not presume to attempt any such alteration; the privilege of abnegating divine law was left to His disciples.

In Puritan England the Christian Sabbath was observed with all the restrictions of Judaism but without a tinge of its joys. In Catholic countries it is observed by attending a brief service under pain of mortal sin. And both have missed the whole purpose of Sabbath. For Christians, by demanding almost normal social services on Sabbath, have deprived a very large section of their co-religionists of their rightful day of rest. True, extra time off may be given in lieu of Sunday, but that is not the same thing. The Christian Sunday can no longer claim in any sense to fulfil the purpose for which God decreed the observance of Sabbath. The very word "Sabbath" means "rest".

It would be a great mistake not to include among the various purposes of Sabbath the important function of drawing the family close together. I am convinced there would be fewer broken homes and divorces, less juvenile delinquency, and a smaller number of frustrated minds, if only Sabbath were sincerely observed. For the non-Jew, the arrival of Sunday often means simply sleeping late that morning, loafing about in old clothes until evening, and then spending the night looking for amusement in the movie houses, the local tavern, or with the T.V. set at home. The Gentile youth is rarely to be found at home on Sunday, and it is seldom that his family is united in any form of religious service.

How different is it in the Jewish home! There on Friday night, the Eve of Sabbath, the mother is busily occupied preparing the house for the great festivity. Even in a poor Jewish home—and there are many impoverished Jews—there is a profusion of special dishes. The candles burn on the table, and the father, with his sons and daughters around him, recites the blessings and drinks the *kiddush* * wine. The meal is full of joy, and the family sings those grand Hebrew melodies which tell of God's bounty and goodness to their fathers and their fathers before them.

When night falls on Saturday the family joins in a most beautiful farewell service to Sabbath, the bride they so gladly welcomed the previous evening. They regret that she has left them; but rejoicing in the new strength her brief sojourn has imparted, they wish one another a "good week".

* Kosher wine for religious use, made from the pure grape and prepared under the supervision of the Beth Din.

Such is the traditional Sabbath in the bosom of the family, and its restoration, in its true and original form as given to us by God, would do much to bring peace, tranquillity, and health of mind and body to a weary and sadly disillusioned world. Sabbath, our sages tell us, is a brief but genuine foretaste of the happiness of the world to come.

The gradual introduction of the five-day week will, I am sure, prove a real blessing to Jew and Gentile alike. Provided men work industriously and honestly on the remaining days, nothing but good can come from extended relaxation. The problem of leisure and its proper use will be a matter of great concern to the educationalist. Our children will enter into a world where they will have time not only to "stand and stare", but also to sit and think. A richer life should result, especially if one full day is dedicated to spiritual rest and refreshment.

I have given considerable space to this particular matter of Sabbath observance, but the fact is that life in a Jewish community differs fundamentally from any other. The entire set of values is different, and the conception of existence in general cannot be compared with any that I have experienced elsewhere or, for that matter, could even have imagined. The Jew regard his religion as an hour-by-hour way of life. Mass once a week, plus occasional duties, could never satisfy his notion of obligation to his Creator. Eating, working, sleeping, and every other phase of life—all these are linked to religion by appropriate blessing and dedications.

For myself, I found the daily practice of Judaism perfectly natural and yet sublime. As time went on I came to feel just the same as any other Jew, free now from that earlier sensation of being a "stranger". I regarded myself, in fact, as being as good a Jew as most, and perhaps a better one than many. I had learned to take a knock and give one in return. Whereas a few years ago I had been afraid of every eye cast upon me, I arrived at a point where I found myself pulling apart certain aspects of Anglo-Jewry and thoroughly enjoying the pastime—a pastime in which, as my readers may possibly have guessed, I still engage without fear or favour where circumstances seem to call for it. But let no non-Jew criticize the Community in my presence, or he will soon know precisely where my sympathies lie.

More and more I found complete composure of soul and spiritual unity in my new faith and way of life. These perpetual conflicts of mind, heart, and soul which had so grievously tormented me in my former sphere had been exercised by the undivided union with God I now experienced. The mind was happy that it had no incompatible acts of faith to accept; the heart was at peace because it was no longer split; and the soul soared aloft to Him no longer obstructed by a dissipation of prayer offered to more than The One Being. I felt that the King and Father of the universe was now the centre of my life and that no barrier existed any more to diminish the bond of union between Creator and creature, between the King and His subject. In short, I knew that the peace of mind which I had found was of a permanent nature, it being rooted in a faith which presented no conflict to my mind. Although Judaism was a revealed religion—the oldest, in fact, of the directly revealed faiths—I could discover in it nothing which, though above reason, was contrary thereto, nothing which offended my conception of God. . . .

I found, too, in the serene, untroubled atmosphere of my new faith, that I was able to meditate more objectively upon so many questions that had harassed me at one time or another in the past, and in many cases to arrive at more rational answers than had formerly characterized my thinking. There was, for example, that everlasting problem of evil. It is a problem as old as the hills, or at all events as old as the Psalmist. Over and over again in his inspired verses of the Psalms, we find the recurrent question, "Why do the righteous suffer and the evil prosper?" And with the Hebraic optimism which I now recognized as being so amply justified the answer always returns to the unshaken conviction that in the end the evildoer vanishes from the face of the earth and is cut off in the midst of his transgression.

Youth, of course, not having had the opportunity of observing a lifetime of adjustment in the scales of justice, is, as I have said elsewhere, frequently troubled to the point of despair by this ever-recurrent problem. And perhaps it is better to admit unhesitatingly and quite honestly that it is a problem without any mathematically precise solution. For "Who hath known the mind of the Lord, or searched the counsels of the Almighty?"

There is, however, one important factor which is frequently overlooked in the discussion of this vexed question. It must be conceded that the Creator has made man equipped with a free will, it being irrelevant whether we approve of this arrangement or not. Granting that it is so, it is clear that man is free to choose between right and wrong. The consequences of exercising this freedom are bound to produce either happiness or misery, not only for the person himself but also for the society in which he lives. For better or for worse, man is a social being, and his conduct cannot but influence the life of his neighbours; it is within his power to make them happy or miserable by his words and actions. But the religious man has God's assurance that all things will be rectified by the Just Judge in the end of days. Thus ran my ruminations, bringing me inevitably to that rock-firm conviction of the Psalmist already quoted—a conviction without which life would for most people become altogether impossible.

Another oft-encountered question upon which I could now bring an unshackled mind to bear was that of why God does not prevent some evil thing which He knows will happen in the future. The answer at which I arrived rests on the very important premise that God does not see or know in what we call "future". There is no such thing as future with God. Everything is *now* to Him. With our idea of time, it is difficult for us to realize that the past and the future are every bit as real as the present—that they are, indeed, one and the same thing as the present. God might be said to see everything in time as well as in space from the top of the mountain, as it were, whereas we on the ground see things only from one angle at a time.

Realizing as I did that my contentment with Judaism was a stabilizing factor in my life and destined to be permanent, I gave much thought in those days to the factors which might account for some Jews not sharing in my satisfaction. My experience of those who drifted from Judaism convinced me fully of one thing at all events; namely, that their revolt was based on the emotion rather than on reason. The vast majority of such people did not embrace another religion; they became nominal Communists, Agnostics, or just plain materialists. Only a negligible minority embraced Catholicism or Anglicanism.

Those who became Catholics must, I surmised, have taken that step in the attempt to find a mental retreat and a dispensation from the struggle of personal responsibility; for obviously a Jew must have already become very assimilated before he could entertain, still less embrace, such doctrines as Transubstantiation (bread and wine being transformed into the body and blood of Jesus), Confession, veneration of saints and their images, or any other of the dogmas which necessitate the suspension of reason if not its utter capitulation. I have encountered only two such cases. One was an embittered and an extreme neurotic, while the other one had received no Jewish education since the age of six.

The considerable number of Jews converted, or rather perverted, to Communism is more readily understood. Communism is the perversion of a Jewish ideal: namely, the Messianic Age. It is a fundamental tenet of Judaism that Messiah will usher in the Era of Justice. The founders of Communism, however, were in no mood to wait for the coming of Messiah. They had before them the object-lesson of too many religious people of all creeds who cared nothing for the sufferings of the masses, but promised the "pie in the sky" while leaving millions of their fellow-creatures to starve. The argument was a potent one in those times, though now with our Welfare State in England it is, of course, harder to appreciate the vehemence of the hunger marchers and street-corner orators of the twenties and thirties.

Bad social conditions are a breeding-ground for Communism, which grows best on hopeless soil. It is a materialistic "religion", it is a denial of faith and revelation. There are no morals in Communism. If the Communist attitude happens to coincide with some particular Commandment or moral precept it is only because it is useful or convenient at that particular juncture. If a Communist state condemns murder or theft that is for the sake of discipline, not in the interests of humanity, and still less because it offends man's Creator. Nor have Communists any regard for truth as an absolute value or virtue. If it chances to be convenient to lie, then lies are good. If murder is the most effective solution to a problem, then murder is no longer a crime, and condonation may even extend to a wholesale massacre.

For a Jew to embrace Communism he will have to accept a common misconception. He assumes it is a Jewish belief that we should simply fold our arms and wait until the Messiah comes. And assuming this, he becomes impatient and seeks a short cut, though short cuts, as history demonstrates, are dangerous. His assumption is, of course, utterly erroneous. Judaism urges justice here and now. It strongly opposes postponement of justice until we get to Heaven.

Unless we work for justice now, the Messianic Era will be delayed. It can only be hastened by our own good works. There are Jews—far too many, I fear—who seem to imagine that so long as the United Synagogue is not in the red all is well with humanity. Such smug little people antagonize many and drive the feebler souls into the arms of materialism. If religious Jews were only a little more worried about their fellow-men we should have fewer defections.

Materialism is, of course, no alternative to religion. And actually, the doctrine of dialectical materialism, as such, appeals to very few, while those who do profess it either live an extremely detached and rarified intellectual existence or, as is more commonly the case, live one life in their study and another in the street. They resemble the Idealist School of Philosophy of the eighteenth and nineteenth centuries, who taught that you cannot know things as they really are, but whose adherents conducted their business life on a very different supposition.

Christianity, has I fear, done much damage in this regard. It has placed too much stress on the rewards of Heaven and too little on justice in Main Street of any town. Christianity, in fact, has swung too far in the direction of other-worldliness, while Communism, on the other hand, has tried to establish Heaven without the aid of the One who alone can build the perfect Kingdom. Judaism represents the rational solution to a spiritual-cum-material problem. While emphasizing the religious aspect of man's destiny, it yet urges constant and strenuous effort towards establishing the reign of justice here and now for all men, Jew and Gentile alike.

One of the most serious charges against Communism is its disregard for the human personality—a disease from which all forms of totalitarianism suffer. The State, which naturally means the ruling group, is considered the all-important factor; all else must serve its ends. The citizen is a mere cog in the machine; neither his body nor his soul can he call his own. Notwithstanding this inhuman attitude, however, intellectual Communism has certain tenets which do appeal to men of humanitarian outlook, since it visualizes all men as brothers living and working in peace. This goes far to explain why so many Jews, with their inborn Messianic ideals and consuming love of justice, have been drawn into the Communist movement. But for most of them this step has in practice involved renunciation of all moral and spiritual ideals. A few, living still in the culture of the Western world, have found it possible to evolve a compromise.

Communism, possessing no means of catering for the higher faculties of man's nature, is bound to fail as a voluntary way of life. Only by force and the establishment of a quasi-police state can it entrench itself in society. The sole alternative soil for its growth is that of instability or despair. True, there are certain countries in Europe where political or semi-intellectual Communism enjoys periodic success. But those countries are notes for caprice and a lack of moral and religious stability.

The Jew who knows his Judaism and is strong enough not to be diverted by unworthy co-religionists, even though they be of the "religious" category, will find in his faith all that he needs for the social, moral, and spiritual salvation of himself and his fellow-men. For in Judaism we have a basic religion capable of satisfying the requirements of every heart and establishing more and more firmly a reign of justice here in this world until the Messiah, with His Own advent, shall assure the perfect state on earth. Every other -ism is unable to provide that.

12

Destination Reached—Mission Beginning

"Mine eyes have seen the glory of the coming of the Lord."

Battle Hymn of the Republic, JULIA WARD HOWE

"Sorrow and misery, in hovels and palaces, in cities and states awaken a yearning and hope for the Messiah in every human breast. It is not the Jewish salvation alone which depends on the resurrection of Zion."

Judaism Eternal, Vol. 1, 139, S. R. HIRSCH (13 (*b*))

PROMINENT among the features of my new faith which most enchanted me was the sonorous and majestic quality of the Jewish prayers. Those prayers I found inspiring above any that I had hitherto known. They lifted one's entire being up to God the Creator and gave a depth of satisfaction I had not realized it possible to experience. I joined with all observant Jews in putting on the tephilling every morning—the leather band a Jew is bidden to wrap around his arm and hand and head. No need for priest or even Pope here—but the direct contact between the servant and his Creator. What a sharp twist of fate, to be reciting the same prayers now, which the founder of Christianity recited some two thousand years ago. I had completed the full circle. I had returned home.

Listening awe-stricken to those splendid, ancient supplications, it became abundantly clear to me that Christians could not possibly achieve a real understanding of their own religion unless they knew a great deal about Jewish practice. The Psalms, used by clergy and congregations in all Christian services, came of course mainly from David, that wise Jewish king and sage. And the prophets, whose writings had contributed so richly to Christian literature, had been Judaism's predominant champions. How much, I reflected, each of the daughter religions of Judaism, Christianity and Islam, owed to their Mother Faith, and how little of it they deigned to acknowledge! Not only had the daughters, and above all the elder daughter, Christianity, failed to render thanks to their mother; they had grossly ill-treated her.

If the Jewish prayers made so deep an impression upon me,

what were my sensations on becoming acquainted with the beauty and grandeur of the Great Festivals! These portray more than anything else, perhaps, the Jewish way of life and outlook. For me, it was as though thousands of years had rolled back and I stood with the worshippers at Sinai or in the Temple. We used to read that Jesus went up to the Festivals, and we know that he himself followed no faith other than that which they interpreted and celebrated.

With the coming of autumn, the Jews of the world prepare for their New Year and Atonement observances. Throughout their long exile in the *Diaspora* * or galut they have accustomed themselves to observing two consecutive New Year days. But it is at the Festivals that the Bible comes to life and Moses walks again. Any Jew who fails to keep the New Year is indeed a weak vessel, but he who neglects the Day of Atonement has already become a stranger to his kind.

The autumn Festivals continue over a span of almost a month, and for every Jew they constitute a period of the most intense heart-searching. During New Year and Atonement the Jew believes that he is in process of being judged, and in synagogues all over the world, whether in times of persecution or of freedom, a mighty appeal soars up to Heaven that the King and Father of mankind may show compassion and mercy to His unworthy children.

The arrival of the New Year is ushered in by the blowing of the *Shofar*, the ram's horn, just such an instrument as has been used in the Temple and by David on the hillsides when calling in his flock. At its penetrating note an intense thrill is felt throughout the congregation, and the solemnity of life and death becomes a reality to souls upon whom the dust of materialism may have gathered thickly since the last Atonement Day. Tradition has it that its origin dates back to Abraham's willingness to observe any and all of God's wishes—even to the point of sacrificing his only son. But

* A comprehensive term denoting all the Jews outside of Israel and scattered throughout the world.

since God wanted only to test Abraham's trust in Him, and not the human sacrifice, He showed him the ram whose horns were enmeshed in the brush. And Abraham sacrificed the ram instead. Ever since the horn of the Ram, the Shofar, has been blown so that Jews may awaken from their slumber, ponder their duty and obligations, their shortcomings and failures, and return from their evil ways. Realizing the symbolic meaning of its origin, a better object for dedication and self-sacrifice could hardly be found.

On that day all Jews fast strictly from sunset to sunset. Neither a crumb of food nor a sip of water passes their lips. And during the whole period of more than twenty-four hours ceaseless prayer for mercy ascends to Heaven. But towards the end of this time of High Festival comes a happy occasion called the Rejoicing of the Law, when children and parents dance round the scrolls of the Law in thanksgiving for the gift of the Commandments at the hands of Moses.*

When the children of Israel were performing their long, weary journey through the wilderness they frequently gazed up through the openings in their tent-tops and beheld the stars. Jews commemorate this by erecting, as bidden in Scripture, temporary structures beside their houses or on their verandahs, where they eat during part of the Sukkoh or Tabernacle Festival. This recalls the journeys of their forefathers and God's preservation of the latter throughout Israel's difficult and often perilous history, and signifies the Jews' complete willingness to trust God without the safety of his four walls insulating him from the vagaries of the weather.

At the time when the Christian world is celebrating Easter, on the other hand, the Jew is reliving, in a truly picturesque and fascinating form, his ancestors' deliverance from their Egyptian bondage. Passover is a favourite family festival. The first two nights are called *Seder* Nights, when the family, together with a number of guests—and a stranger is often invited to participate—sit around the table and read or sing a

* See Supplementary Reading Matter (14), p. 238.

special service which relates the history of Moses and the Israelites' escape from their slavery under the Egyptian Pharaoh. The Plagues and all the other circumstances of the Exodus are most vividly retold.

The various kinds of food served at the Passover meal are symbolic of the whole historical drama. The roasted lamb-bone represents the Paschal Lamb which was sacrificed on the Eve of Passover. Then there is a special mixture called *Charosis*, made of apples, nuts, wine, sugar, and cinnamon. Brown in colour, it is intended to remind us of the bricks which our ancestors were forced to make for their Egyptian taskmasters. Horseradish calls to mind the slavery, and a roasted egg represents the bone Festival sacrifice in the Temple in Jerusalem—now destroyed. On another tray are set out the three *Matsos*, the unleavened cakes. An extremely important person on Passover Night is the family's youngest child. It is he or she who asks the traditional Questions concerning the flight from the house of bondage.

How often, down through the centuries, have we witnessed further deliverances of Israel from persecutors determined to obliterate her. Within sight of utter extinction, as in the last great war, she has been snatched from the fires of hatred. Hitler left no stone unturned to annihilate the entire race: six million were massacred in the space of five years. And yet, as, year after year, each Passover Night returns on the calendar, there remains a remnant to continue into history the song of thanksgiving for God's everlasting love and protection extended to His people.

Let us never forget how within a few months of the arch-fiend Hitler's death the seemingly impossible had happened. Just when Israel seemed blotted out for ever, she arose as an island of refuge and beacon of hope to inspire those who until then had been all but submerged in despair. It was a major miracle, one of which we have yet to prove ourselves deserving. We must surely trust that those who populate that divinely restored homeland will not be the last to render gratitude!

I have always regarded the establishment of the State of Israel as a vital though only very preliminary step towards the advent of the Messianic Age. Even as a Christian I had been a sincere Zionist, but today, needless to say, my attitude towards Zionism is immeasurably reinforced. Judaism and Zionism go hand in hand. And I am not referring to the purely political Zionism of the Israeli nationalist, but to the Zionism of the Bible.

The modern miracle of Israel's creation and survival brings home to us most forcibly the words of the prophet Amos:

"And I will turn the captivity of my people of Israel,
And they shall build the waste cities and inhabit them;
And they shall plant vineyards, and drink the wine thereof;
They shall also make gardens, and eat the fruit of them.
And I will plant them upon their land, and they shall be
no more plucked up out of the land which I have given them,
Saith the Lord thy God."

Israel is, and always will be, an absolute necessity for Jewish survival. Apart from the six million of our people murdered in Europe, there were thousands upon thousands more, with the entire foundations of their lives in ruins, who had no place to which to flee—and all this within our own lifetime. But for century after century before our era the Jew, simply because he was a Jew, had been hounded from one country to another and found no peace. Deprived of the right to enter those professions in which he naturally excelled, such as medicine, law, and the arts, he was compelled to seek his livelihood in fields less pleasant. And having forced him into this anomalous and invidious status, what did the Gentile world then do but abuse him for being in that situation! Death and torture, long years in prison, confinement to overcrowded tenements in slums of towns and cities, and finally Hitler's charnel-houses, left the Jew the world's pariah, despised for those very characteristics which the world itself had forced him to evolve. There was an underlying sting in the sly remark of that waggish bishop who once observed that "we owe the Jews more than we can ever pay them!"

It seems a peculiarly cruel twist of fate whereby one of the most cultured of all races should be regarded as materialistic and solely concerned with finance. And the accusation is all the more cruel in view of the fact that the Jewish minority became associated with monetary interests only as the direct result of the persistent and organized persecution which barred them from the universities and the learned professions.

How grievous, moreover, was the world's own loss through that very exclusion of the Jew from the callings he was so admirably qualified to practise and adorn! Since their emancipation a little more than a century ago, Jews have been worthily represented in law, medicine, teaching, and certain of the arts to an extent quite out of proportion to their numbers. Indeed, the majority of young Jews today aspire to professions rather than to commercial pursuits. And their parents, let it be added, frequently make considerable sacrifices to send them to university, preferring that they should follow a more distinguished, though possibly less lucrative, calling rather than enter the family business.

Certainly I myself have found that the Jewish people have an atmosphere and tradition of culture which shows every sign of being very deeply rooted. The poorest Jewish boy from the East End of London is, in my experience, an aristocrat in his own right. It may well be that the air of self-conscious superiority to be discerned in certain Jewish people is a source of irritation to some Gentiles, but in most cases there is no deliberate intention to be aggressive. Rather is it a natural and spontaneous reaction to the fact that the positive contributions to civilization made by the Jewish race are either ignored by the world at large or, at any rate, taken for granted.

It is common knowledge, of course, how immense has been the part played by Jews in the development of the theatre, screen, and kindred artistic media; but in the spheres of graphic and architectural art their rôle has been more restricted, due no doubt to the necessity in past centuries of stressing the monotheistic aspect of their faith. For even today there are many religious Jews who disapprove of human beings' depictment in pictorial art or sculpture, lest their images become objects of undue devotion, as so specifically prohibited in the Third Commandment.

On the other hand, however, a third-century synagogue has recently been discovered in an excellent state of preservation with its walls richly adorned with frescoes depicting biblical scenes and bearing a remarkable resemblance to Early Christian art. Much of the inspiration of European art, in fact, sprang from Jewish sources. Rembrandt, for example, was certainly influenced to a very considerable degree by the Jews among whom he lived. It has even been suggested, indeed, that he was himself of Jewish origin, but there is no documentary evidence in support of this theory.

Although Jews, partly from the religious considerations already cited or because of social prejudice, have not produced in the realm of pictorial art the results they have achieved elsewhere, the Jewish tradition, particularly as drawn from biblical sources, has none the less given birth to many brilliant masterpieces. Marc Chagall, that venerable Jewish modern painter, has achieved great fame all over the world. His paintings are all deeply rooted in Jewish mysticism.

It is in the sphere of music that Jews have long taken an outstandingly prominent part, and it is interesting today to note the high percentage of our race to be found in all leading orchestras both in England and abroad. Turning, too, to composers, we have the brilliant example of Mendelssohn, a baptized Jew, and the tremendous influence he has exercised upon the Gentile world through his magnificent oratorio the "Elijah". He makes the prophet live again and brings home to us with an inspiring realism the scenes enacted upon Mount Carmel. Consider also the great number of Jewish instrumentalists, so numerous that space will not permit their names to be listed here; to take just a few examples, Kreisler, Menuhin, Solomon, Myra Hess, Elmen, Heifetz, Rubenstein—all of these have brought a rich contribution to contemporary music and established their names in the annals of posterity. And as conductor, Leonard Bernstein has risen to great fame, not only in America, where he conducts the New York Symphony Orchestra, but all over the world. What an immense contribution by a persecuted people.

It is perhaps in the sphere of medicine, however, that the Jewish gift to humanity has been most marked of all. From the time of Maimonides until the present day Jews have served mankind either as physicians or as surgeons, while many have made discoveries which have resulted in the lessening of suffering and the hastening of healing. It seems a shameful paradox that a minority which has taken part so keenly in the conquest of disease and pain should itself have been subjected to such a ruthless and unremitting persecution throughout the ages.

The Jewish love of medical practice springs from biblical laws. Indeed the Bible itself might almost be described as a text-book of racial and personal hygiene, as may be seen on reference to the Book of Deuteronomy. The Jewish rules of ritual cleanliness were, and still are, in a more modern form, wonderful safeguards against disease and pestilence. The Jews, after all, were leading an extremely hygienic existence when most of Europe and Asia still remained in the darkness of primitive dirt and contagion. And even during times of persecution certain brilliant physicians of Jewish origin were kept at the courts of anti-Semitic princes.

Moses Maimonides, court physician in Egypt in the eleventh century, had, both as a doctor and as a philosopher and scholar of profound erudition, achieved a place in world history seldom surpassed. It has, in fact, been said with much truth that "from Moses to Moses there was none like Maimonides". The richness and fullness of his life make the records of many other famous men seem insignificant by comparison. He was in tremendous demand as a physician, with all classes, from the Islamic ruler to the peasant outcast, clamouring alike for his services. His psychological approach to medicine placed him well in advance of his age, and he was also a great advocate of preventive treatment, urging the regular consultation of doctors during periods of good health.

In the sphere of medical discovery, too, the Jewish race has contributed more than its proportionate share. In our own day we have the example of the latest and most revolutionary discovery for the prevention and cure of polio by Dr. Salk, an American Jew.

In still yet other fields, and notably in that of world affairs, we have witnessed the wonderful achievements of such men as Dr. Weizmann, Viscount Samuel, Lord Reading, and others too numerous to mention. Britain, because of her favourable attitude towards all minorities, especially persecuted minorities, has been well served by patriotic Jews in all branches of national life. One of her greatest Prime Ministers, Benjamin Disraeli, was of Jewish origin, and his work for Britain, the adopted land he loved so well, has yet to receive full recognition. For although it is his work in foreign affairs that is most widely known and acclaimed, Disraeli also undertook a considerable number of social reforms in the interests of the poorer classes. He was, in point of fact, one of the first Tories to advocate such measures in an effective manner.

During Hitler's unspeakable persecution hundreds of Jewish scholars, scientists, and medical men who had contrived to make miraculous escapes from death settled in Britain and other democratic countries, where they dedicated their talents to the service of their deliverers. It can truthfully be said, in fact, that Hitler, by driving out these men, helped to forge the weapon for his own destruction.

Despite all these manifold contributions to the cause of civilization, however, the contribution for which the world in general must ever remain most indebted to the Jewish people is the inspired work of the prophets and psalmists. So many races and religions, alas, have made the thoughts of such men as David and Elijah their own while often forgetting the source from which they sprang!

The great achievements of the Jewish race which I have here attempted to recall in brief outline seem to me to make it doubly imperative that the Judaism of today should, without fear or favour, undertake a candid survey to determine its own deficiencies and weaknesses and, that done, seek forthwith to discover and apply the appropriate remedies. It is not enough to deplore the fact that some 70 per cent of contemporary Jews appear to display an irreligious attitude, nor to attempt to excuse their apathy on the grounds that approximately 60 per cent of the British general public, and 40 per cent of that of America, are living their lives with no definite religious affiliation and show no signs of shedding this indifference.

Looking at the situation from a general and altruistic standpoint, it would seem that what is urgently needed is a vast religious revival, some sort of "moral re-armament" movement sponsored jointly by all the world's great religions, though of that there appears but little hope in the foreseeable future. If in war-time the nations and the various denominations can come together to serve the common weal, why cannot they do so in these so-called days of peace, when the position is no less perilous, though in a different sense? Surely it is religion rather than politics that should forge the instruments of peace. But alas, the world appears to have no leaders great enough to grasp this truth and take their stand thereon.

Jewry cannot, in any case, afford to wait for any such world-wide upsurge of faith. Jewry must act independently to set its house in order. And what better time than in this present era, when the Jewish people, after living through centuries scattered to the four corners of the earth and subjected to untold torments and disabilities, have gained at last a homeland they can truly call their own—a homeland, moreover, won by the blood and toil and sweat of their own kind? The actual establishment of the State of Israel was brought about, under Providence, by the epic struggle of its youth, a youth which poured out its blood in rich abundance and gained a victory against staggering odds. As in Bible days, a few were able, by the hand of the Lord, to prevail against a mighty host.

I remember so well the day that the State of Israel was established. I was sitting in the office of the Senior Chaplain to the Jewish Forces, now Chief Rabbi. I was explaining to him my serious personal problem, and found in him a most sympathetic friend. I remember his saying that the Jews "rejoiced with trembling" at this wonderful thing which had come to pass. It seemed too good to be true.

Upon Jewry lies the solemn obligation to be worthy of that wonderful thing. In these anxious days we need constantly to remind ourselves of the Promises made to our forefathers and the condition attached to those Promises: namely, the faithful adherence of our people to Torah. Nationalism is not enough! If we permit Zionism to be divorced from Judaism, we are building on shifting sands and copying the errors of our worst enemies—the materialist nationalists. Israel can choose between becoming once again a light unto the nations or reverting to a rôle of mediocrity among dozens of minor states whose only mission is to expand that which has no lasting value.

But outside Israel, too, there is materialism to be combated if we are to prosper. I wrote earlier of the form of materialism for which Communism stands. I am thinking now of another materialism equally insidious and by far the most common, the one which claims the great majority of those who drift from Judaism. It is what we may term "good time" materialism. Most young Jews who have lost their religious identity have not given allegiance to Marxism or any other "ism". They are not particularly averse to institutional Judaism, but they have scarcely heard of the United Synagogue and probably could not name the Chief Rabbi. They neither know nor care what is expected of them, though that is more our fault than theirs, since we have been overly busy with the righteous.

Dancing, films, sport, fashion—these are the things which give those young people a motive for "living". As soon as work is over they make a bee-line for that part of their existence which provides distraction. Personally, I have no patience with those who regard the majority of modern Jewish youth as "bad". Pleasure-loving they are, inclined to be selfish, and without an ideal, but that is all. Their endless round of pleasure and distraction supplies a form of escapism from the terrible problem of life. They indirectly ask us, "What is it all about?" and we give them no reply. Pleasure, as such, has become the new idolatry, and most of us are guilty of worshipping at its shrine, albeit vicariously.

A puritanical crusade against amusement would do more harm than good. What is needed is to direct the healthy desire for a full life into positive channels. Judaism, being the most practical and most rational of all faiths, has a golden opportunity, but it must not ask modern youth to become Talmudic scholars in six months. A gradual process of weaning must take place. A boy or girl who has spent four evenings a week at the Palais de Danse for years on end must be lured with heavily sugar-coated pills. Perhaps their sons will need no sugar, but unless we prescribe for the parent we shall never get near enough to cure the son.

The Communists are prepared to take infinite pains to gain a single recruit, while we, by contrast, are painfully apathetic in regard to our own lost legion. My attitude, I hope I need scarcely say, is not a "missionary" attitude. It is merely fraternal and based on elementary loyalty to flesh and blood, to race and religion.

Many victims of the new materialism come from worldly homes. The parents maintain a nominal relationship with the synagogue and duly burn two candles on Sabbath. They probably also keep a Kosher house, observe Atonement and perhaps Passover as well. But that is all. And the children, for their part, observe a vague external distinction between Sabbath and Sunday, but it is all very transitory, very unreal. The parents are reluctant to push religion, even supposing they had it to push. Perhaps the grandparents overpushed it. We can only hope that when this midsummer madness has passed we may settle down to a *via media*—Orthodoxy without tears!

The problem of the non-attached Jewish child arising from divorce, sickness, or death of parents must receive priority. A good boarding school such as Carmel College provides the satisfactory solution. And I most fervently hope that advantage will come to be widely taken of that solution as facilities increase. My main concern as a Jew is precisely what it was in my former religious environment—unattached youth. We have yet to bring to that task the energy, imagination, and resources it so urgently demands.

It is my firm and settled view, now that I have spent several years in an intensive Jewish *milieu*, that the best road for latter-day Jewry is that of traditional Judaism, wherein the two extremes of fanaticism and Liberalism are avoided. It is by way of the *via media*, I am convinced, that world-Jewry will return and find its social, spiritual, and moral salvation through a sane, vital, and living Judaism. Is it too much to hope that this path may lead ultimately to a point where the importance of the modern Jew will be gauged by the traditional standards of character and culture rather than by the now so disgustingly prevalent yard-stick of his bank balance?

Apart from the problems presented by non-attached Jewish youth and by materialism, one of the chief dangers for Anglo-Jewry lies, I consider, in the ever-increasing volume of mixed marriages. By this I mean, of course, the unions between Jews and non-Jewish partners. A marriage which takes place after the reception of the non-Jewish party into the faith is, I need hardly say, a Jewish marriage. The Beth Din, as a rule, will not receive a non-Jew into the Community unless it is very clear indeed that there is a strong and sincere desire for the faith itself, and not simply for the other party. Such sincerity is severely tested by prolonged delays, lasting often for as much as several years.

When a Jew marries a Gentile he or she is betraying our people and all our traditions. Mixed marriages are our greatest curse; in our long history we have had no more dangerous enemy. The children of such unions are placed in a false position. They often finish up by detesting all religion in general, and Judaism in particular, because they have become outcasts.

Unfortunately many of our leaders seem to be afraid to speak out boldly against this communal cancer. Not only do they fail to cry "Wolf", but they actually welcome the enemy to the point where he no longer bothers to assume sheep's clothing. We must, perhaps, write off many of the last generation as losses, but we can at least do something to safeguard the future. As Chief Rabbi Brodie said when he became the leader of British Jewry, "It is not sufficient to preach against mixed marriages: we must provide our Jewish youth with facilities which will keep them together."

No positive step towards carrying out this advice of Chief Rabbi Brodie's has been taken as yet, and concerning mixed marriages it is essential that something *should* be done. It may happen that two or three out of a hundred such unions prove successful, but their success is always at the expense of Judaism. They serve as a deceptive model for the weak of spirit, and we hear nothing more concerning the leakage resulting from the infinitely greater number of failures. The young apostates become entirely assimilated to the non-Jewish world, a total loss to the Mother Faith. A few there are who come back in later generations of their own accord, but at a terrible cost, as some of us have reason to know.

Lest the attitude of Judaism in this matter be considered

singular, it should be remembered that the Catholic Church, too, has long recognized the serious loss sustained through mixed marriages. As I have previously pointed out, she will grant dispensations for such unions only on strict conditions relating to the Catholic upbringing of any offspring. Indeed, she goes farther than that, inasmuch as the Catholic party to the marriage is urged to seek the conversion of the non-Catholic partner. Judaism, however, recognizes no system of dispensations. Since intermarriage is contrary to the Law, no mortal being can grant a dispensation for it. We may neither add to the Law of Moses nor subtract therefrom.

Until we set our Anglo-Jewish house in order in respect of the several weaknesses I have here indicated, I cannot see on what grounds we can claim to be truly worthy of the agonizing birth-throes that brought the State of Israel into being. The argument, sometimes encountered, that effort and money are being diverted into ensuring the continued welfare of Israel does not, in my view, cut any ice. Few are more keenly Zionist than I, but I strongly condemn any notion that the educational and social needs of the *Diaspora* must be shelved in order to build Israel in a day. Whether we like it or not, the majority of Jews will remain in their adopted lands for some time to come. The stronger and more influential we are in those adopted lands, the more efficacious will be our efforts on behalf of Israel.

At the present stage influence is almost as important as money, and we have reached a point where they are by no means synonymous. The parochial mentality which leads so many English Jews to imagine they have saved, or will save, Israel by putting an extra shilling in the collection-box has surely proved itself worthless. Israel does undeniably need money, plus every other form of material support we can give at present, but she needs above all the weight of public opinion from as many Jews and non-Jews as can be marshalled to her aid. Israel's enemies can procure more money and still more tanks. The final issue will depend upon the help of the Lord and the moral support of the nations. The more highly respected we in the *Diaspora* become, the more help shall we be able to bring to Israel, the land which the Lord God has given to us and to our children for ever, and in which it must be the ardent desire of all Jews not as yet too aged eventually to settle.

Israel has given a sense and security to the remaining Jews of the *Diaspora*. Already it has provided a home for millions. If not all can find a home there as yet, at least they have a spiritual and cultural centre. They can visit it with the knowledge that there, at all events, is a place on the earth belonging to them even as it belonged aforetime to their forefathers, Abraham, Isaac, and Jacob.*

Let us pray with all our hearts that never again will the Jews receive at the hands of the nations such diabolical treatment as they have suffered in past centuries and in our own times; that Israel may henceforth be allowed to work out her destiny in unbroken peace. The concentration camps have been too easily forgotten. Had six millions of any other race been treated with such savagery, the world's memory would not have been so short. The Jew will not forget—nor should he. What is more important, He that keepeth Israel will not forget. The Jew has many sins to answer for, but His God does not regard lightly the persecutions undergone at the hands of the nations. Many great and powerful people have oppressed Israel in the past, but time has shown that they have not escaped punishment.

What, then, of the ultimate future? Before my imagination, when I allow it to run uncurbed, stretches a dazzling vista. The world now feels, and will increasingly feel, that God has not altogether deserted His chosen ones. And as that realization grows, so will the influence of Israel among the nations increase and continue to increase, be very sure of that. Already she has won respect, already her diplomatic representatives are found in many of the world's capitals. Nevertheless, we must beware of letting ourselves be tempted

* See Supplementary Reading Matter (15), p. 238.

into undue optimism, as some are being tempted, in what concerns the extension of that influence in the religious sphere. It is obvious that a very lengthy interval—many centuries long, possibly—must elapse before the Mother Faith, old, travel-worn, and deeply scarred, can hope to regain her full and rightful measure of world-influence. That will not happen until the coming of the Messianic Age, when peace, justice, and the true faith, founded on an all-consuming passion for God's unity and free of every barrier between man and his Creator, shall be established by the true Messiah. Then, and then only, the light will surely spread until, in some century of the far future, the whole world shall adore no other name but that of Him who made heaven and earth and all that in them is.

And now, with that divine ray of assurance glowing in my inmost heart, the time has come for me to bring this writing to a close. My strange path has often been a lonely one, sometimes a path strewn with obstructions calling for more courage to face than I could ever have supposed myself to command. Have I, in venturing into the realm of prophecy concerning an era of enlightenment seemingly infinitely remote, presumed too far? Only time can tell. I can but add that this vision of ultimate world-acceptance of the Mother Faith was already with me when, as a proselyte, I was summoned to the traditional Reading of the Law and heard myself called, in accordance with ancient usage, by the name of "Abraham, the son of Abraham", a title before which, I felt, the most exalted names in heraldry paled into insignificance. And back to my mind, as so often before, came that exhortation of my schoolmaster, "Aim at the stars and nothing lower."

Let this, then, be my Nunc Dimittis: To Jew and Gentile alike, *Shalom!*—"Peace!" How true ring the words of that ancient Psalmist of Israel, when he sings in the 117th Psalm:

> "O praise the Lord, all ye Nations; laud him all ye peoples. For his lovingkindness is mighty over us; and the truth of the Lord endureth for ever. Praise ye the Lord."

Epilogue

THE question has frequently been asked, "How do you feel, after seven years in Jewry?"

I can sincerely reply that I have never enjoyed such peace of heart and contentment of mind in my life. There have been serious problems, and difficulties of adjustment, but they have been pinpricks above the surface.

I did not forsake family, friends, the dignity of the priesthood, and devoted subjects in order to please any human being, whether Jew or Gentile.

The call to embrace the Mother Faith was as clear to recognize as it was difficult to answer. Only God could ask it.

Not only do I feel confident in my new world, but I have reason to believe that I am more convinced of the truth and value of Judaism than a large percentage of my co-religionists.

My main concern is not for myself, but for Jewry. Here I must confess to a feeling of anxiety and divine discontent with things as they are.

It is my most firm belief that the Almighty has a very vital rôle for His ancient people in the modern world. They have been miraculously preserved for a supreme purpose. That mission is, as of old, to bear witness to the absolute unity of God and the laws which He has revealed to mankind for all time.

Eventually, the Jewish people must bear witness to the truths of which they are the appointed custodians.

As I see the situation, our most vulnerable point is our Jewish youth. Unwilling as our authorities are to recognize the fact, we are losing hundreds of teenagers every year in the great leakage. A very high percentage of our young people are adrift from Jewish life. *The great army of unattached youth is marching from apathy, to apostasy!!* The process will be complete in another ten or twenty years, unless we act quickly. The loss of six million of our brethren was mostly, if not entirely, beyond our control. But our conscience will certainly not be clear, if we permit a whole generation to drift out, with no serious effort on our part to save them. Our efforts at present are all too feeble. Both in New York and London, even in Jerusalem, there is an ever-widening gap between our young Jews and their grandparents. Certain traditions still receive their lip service. They stay home for supper on Friday nights, but then depart for the usual round of entertainment and assimilative recreation.

All youth needs an ideal, and young Jews are no exception to this. Young Catholics have Rome and all the spiritual and moral influence of the Vatican to inspire them.

Providence has granted to our people within our own time a miracle of rebirth which only awaits our full recognition and co-operation.

Twelve years ago, the hope of centuries was realized. The Almighty restored us to the land promised to our Father, Abraham, and his seed for ever. No longer are we a reproach among the nations. We need not wander the earth as exiles. Israel will receive as many as wish to accept her invitation.

Too little is said about Israel in our colleges and schools. Every school and youth club should send an annual party to Israel, to witness this great miracle of the century. Let them see the desert bloom as a rose, and the thorn give way to the myrtle tree, as our sages long ago prophesied.

Tell them that this humanly impossible thing happened, just when the entire Jewish race was at the point of extinction. Men asked, as in the time of David, "Where is now their God?" The establishment of the State of Israel was a miracle. Make that quite clear to our youth. Jewry and

Judaism are no longer complete without the full realization of the place that Israel now holds in relation to both.*

This of necessity involves a re-orientation of our entire Jewish educational system. Even our liturgy needs focusing to envisage this vital and fundamental fact of our history. The prayers of our Fathers have begun to be answered. Why not accept this fact in the prayers we say each day? Why pray as though we were still exiles in the absolute sense?

Our youth is waiting for this message. They want a reason for being Jews, and Israel is half the answer.

Also, let us use the movies, radio, and television to portray to our youth the glories of Jewish history. We are the people of The Book—that Book which has given the world its moral and spiritual standards.

Youth will lose its inferiority complex in relation to Judaism once it realizes what the non-Jewish world also must be taught to realize, viz. that Judaism, the Mother religion, has given to the world: The Commandments, The Psalms, The Prophets. Even the Sermon on The Mount was 75 per cent Judaic in origin and content. Since Jesus sat at the feet of the rabbis, how could it be otherwise?

We shall reap the harvest at present being sown by our Jewish schools, founded within the last two decades. But that harvest will be lost if we fail to gather it in. There must be an efficient youth movement everywhere Jews have settled, which will follow up every boy and girl leaving school. Here is our weak spot. There is no bridge from the school to the synagogue!

Lack of vision, obsolete methods, and petty jealousies prevent the Jewish youth movement from functioning efficiently.

A national council of youth directors, and experienced consultants, must be set up in every part of Jewry. Action must be co-ordinated, and rendered effective.

Another important step is the teaching of Modern Hebrew to all our children and young people. Thus will their tradi-

* See Supplementary Reading Matter (16), p. 238.

tion and culture spring to life, and a living bond of union be forged between Jews all over the world. History, Scripture, and all the treasures of our heritage will become real again—not cold print!

Our youth will realize that they are no longer dead branches of an obsolete tree, but the strong shoots of a new growth which has returned to life, and vigour.

With vision and energy, I know that we can reclaim the drifting masses of youth. But there is not a day to be lost.

Finally, I would call upon every Jew to reflect seriously upon the question "Why am I a Jew?" The answer can be found only in an understanding of why, and for what purpose, the Almighty chose the Jew. To find that answer, each son of Abraham must go back to the Source, The Old Testament, The Mishna, The Talmud, and the Midrash, and study with understanding born of prayer and meditation.

He should reach the certain conclusion, that he is a member of the oldest and greatest aristocracy in history. He should rediscover the vital fact, that the fundamental purpose that God had in mind for the Jew has yet to be fully realized. The world is waiting to be taught that there is indeed but One God.

With God's help our people are due for a spiritual and moral renaissance. Perhaps within our own day we shall see the dead bones of Jewry rise up from the valley of materialism, and clothe themselves with the breath that still flows strongly from Sinai.

In the end of days the Messiah will speak from Jerusalem, and the word of The Lord shall be heard from The Holy City.

May the Jew, who was destined for all time to make a unique contribution to the great and final era of history, prove worthy of his privileged rôle.

Jerusalem, Israel

June, 1960
Sivan, 5720

ADDENDUM A

TWO VIEWS ON PROSELYTIZATION

1. England*

"Probably the most difficult problem facing the Beth Din (otherwise known as the Court of the Chief Rabbi) is proselytisation. In many cases the applicant has married, or is about to marry a Jew who is anxious for the sake of the children or parents, to secure the admission of his non-Jewish partner into Judaism. The Beth Din is frankly alarmed at the high incidence of intermarriage, and applicants for conversion are automatically discouraged. (The present rate of intermarriage is unknown, but in 1953 was estimated to be between ten and twelve per cent. The figure for the provinces are believed to be particularly high.) What is certain is that the number of applications for proselytization have increased in the past three years. Applications in 1958 totalled 137 (of whom 21 were admitted) in 1957 they were 121 (9 admitted) and the previous year 120 (23 admitted). . . .

"What is the Beth Din's attitude to these applications? This is what the Chief Rabbi says: 'We are slow in dealing with these cases. Not many are admitted. We must be sure of their moral and social bona fides before dealing with the religious situation. We must be sure that the applicant is one who really wants to become a Jew. We do not close the door, but we accept only those who convince us that they will genuinely adhere to Judaism. There has been no change in policy in recent years. We handle each application with care and a great sense of responsibility. We must think in terms of the kehilla (community).' In general, according to the Beth Din there is a big gap between the Court's requirements and applicants. In most cases, it says, there is no genuine desire for conversion, and, in this connection, the Dayanim (the 5 'Eccleciastical Assessors' to the Chief Rabbi) emphasize that where mixed marriages break down the proselyte partner almost invariably abandons Judaism.

"But the Beth Din insists that it treats each case on its merits and hears every applicant (last year 315 interviews were granted in proselytization cases. . . . Special consideration, say the

* Extracts from David Pela's article "The Chief Rabbi's Court", which appeared in the *Jewish Chronicle*, London, July 10, 1959.

Dayanim, is given to children of mixed marriages, and they claim, the Court goes out of its way to help these youngsters. If it is satisfied that such children are brought up in an Orthodox atmosphere it will give them priority. . . . But as has been indicated, the Beth Din is strongly against proselytization. They regard this and intermarriage as among the great Jewish social problems of our time. Their attitude is: 'If the community will not support us on this issue, it will undermine all the Jewish communities in Europe, where the situation—regarding intermarriage—is much worse. The community is not aware of the gravity of the problem. . . . We are not too rigid. . . . Intermarriage is the greatest evil. Who gains from encouraging it? Frequently the parents of both partners are against it. The marriages often break down because the partners come from different religions.' "

2. United States

There is no Chief Rabbinate in America, and therefore no Chief Rabbi's Court exists there either. Applicants for proselytization must therefore turn to individual Rabbis, who either discourage or encourage such applicants, depending on whether the Rabbi is a member of the Orthodox, Conservative, or Reform Movement in the United States. No figures similar to those quoted above are available, but I found the following comment in the latest issue of the *American Jewish Yearbook*: *

Proselytism

"There was much writing and preaching about a Jewish missionary effort. Rabbi Robert Gordis (Conservative movement) was a major advocate of proselytization. In an article in the *National Jewish* monthly for March 1958, later given wider publicity in *Time* magazine, Gordis recommended that the leaders of the major Jewish religious organizations get together to consider the possibilities of launching a missionary program among the unaffiliated Gentile population in the Western Hemisphere and Japan. . . . Typical of the opposition to Jewish proselytization was the argument of Rabbi Harold Schulweiss of Oakland, Cal., published in the *Reconstructionist* for October 31, 1958, in which he wrote that missionary efforts implied 'religious superiority', and that Jewish missionaries would do better *to address themselves to Jews who stood outside Judaism*." (Italics mine, not those of the writer.)

* Excerpt from the *American Jewish Yearbook*, Vol. 60, page 64, published by the American Jewish Committee, New York, and the Jewish Publication Society, Philadelphia, 1959.